Talk German

Judith Matthews
and
Jeanne Wood

Series editor
Alwena Lamping

 ACTIVE

In memory of Jeanne Wood, who died shortly before the publication of this book.

BBC Active, an imprint of Educational Publishers LLP, part of the Pearson Education Group
Edinburgh Gate
Harlow
Essex CM20 2JE
England

First published 1998
Reprinted 1999, 2000, 2001 (twice)
Reprinted and updated 2002, 2003, 2004, 2005 (twice)
Second impression 2006
Reprinted 2007

ISBN-13: 978-0-563-52018-4
ISBN-10: 0-563-52018-3

Edited by Naomi Laredo
Additional editing by Carola Hammerer
Design Management by Book Creation Services
Design by Avril Broadley for BCS
Illustrations by Avril Broadley, Sylvie Rabbe and Beatriz Waller for BCS
Typeset by Gene Ferber for BCS
Cover design by Helen Williams and Matt Bookman
Cover photograph Matton Images UK
Audio producer John Green, TEFL tapes
Sound engineer Tim Woolf
Presenters Wolf Kahler, Aletta Lohmeyer, Peter Stark, Getrude Thoma
Studio Robert Nichols Audio Productions
Music by Peter Hutchings
Printed and bound in Great Britain by Martins-the-Printers

The Publisher's policy is to use paper manufactured from sustainable forests.

Contents

Introduction

Welcome to **Talk German**, the BBC's new German course for absolute beginners. Designed for adults, learning at home or in a class, it provides the ideal introduction to German, covering the basic language needed in everyday situations on a visit to Germany, Austria or German-speaking Switzerland. It is suitable if you want to learn for work, for fun and in order to prepare for a first level qualification.

Talk German is an interactive course consisting of a book and two 60-minute audio cassettes or CDs made by native German speakers. Although designed to be used with the audio, the book could be used separately as the audio scripts are included in the reference section. Free tutors support and activities are available at http://www.bbcworldwide.com/talk.

Talk German encourages you to make genuine progress and promotes a real sense of achievement. The key to its effectiveness lies in its structure and its systematic approach. Key features include:

- simple step-by-step presentation of new language
- involvement and interaction at every stage of the learning process
- regular progress checks
- useful hints on study skills and language learning strategies

How to use Talk German

Each of the ten units is completed in ten easy-to-follow steps.

1   Read the first page of the unit to focus on what you are aiming to learn and to note any key vocabulary in the *In Deutschland* section. This provides useful and relevant information on the German-speaking countries and sets your learning in context.

2   Listen to the key phrases on the audio – don't be tempted to read them first. Then listen to them again, this time reading them in your book too. Finally, try reading them out loud before listening one more time.

3   Work your way, step by step, through the activities which follow the key phrases. These highlight key language elements and are carefully designed to develop your listening skills and your understanding of German.

When you hear the activity number, pause the audio and read the instructions before you listen. To check your answers, refer to the *Audio scripts and answers* starting on page 100.

4 Read the *Auf Deutsch* explanations of how the language works as you come to them – they are placed just where you need that information.

5 When you have completed the activities, and before you try the *Put it all together* section, close your book and listen to the German conversations straight through. The more times you listen, the more familiar the language will become and the more comfortable you will become with it. You might also like to read the dialogues at this stage.

6 Complete the consolidation activities on the *Put it all together* page and check your answers with the *Audio scripts and answers*.

7 Use the language you've learnt – the presenters on the audio will prompt you and guide you through the *Now you're talking!* page as you practise speaking German.

8 Check your progress. First, test your knowledge with the quiz. Then check whether you can do everything on the checklist – if in doubt, go back and spend some more time on the relevant section. You'll have further opportunities to test your knowledge in each *Kontrollpunkt* after units 4, 7 and 10.

9 Read the learning hint at the end of the unit, which provides ideas and suggestions on how to use your study time effectively or how to extend your knowledge.

10 Finally, relax and listen to the whole unit, understanding what the people are saying in German and taking part in the conversations. This time you may not need the book so you can listen to the audio on its own.

Viel Glück! Good luck!

Pronunciation guide

Vowels are long	● when doubled or followed by **h**: **Tee**, **Bahn**
	● before a single consonant: **gut**, **Name**, **Straße**
They are short	● before two consonants: **voll**, **und**, **dass**

Here are the German letters and letter combinations that are pronounced differently from English, with approximate English equivalents:

Sound	German example(s)	English equivalent
a (long/short)	Bahnhof/Kaffee	*rather*/*sample* (but shorter)
ä (long/short)	Käse/Kännchen	*late*/*get*
au	Hausfrau, aus	*now*
äu	Fräulein	*oil*
ch (after **a**, **au**, **o**, **u**)	Nacht, auch	*loch*
ch (elsewhere)	ich, nicht	*human*
chs	sechs, nächst	*expel*
e (long/short)	Tee/Geld	*hate*/*met*
ei	drei, mein	*mine*
eu	neun, Deutsch	*foil*
g (in **-ig**)	vierzig	*human*
i (long/short)	Ihnen/bitte	*tree*/*hit*
ie	Sie, Bier	*tree*
ie (at end of word)	Familie	*pannier*
j	ja, Januar	*yet*
o (long/short)	ohne/Post	*oh!*/*lot*
ö (long/short)	schön/möchte	*'her'*/*'men'* spoken with lips pouted
sch	Flasche	*sheep*
sp (at start of word)	Sport	*cashpoint*
ß (**Eszett**)	Straße, heißen	*pass*
st (at start of word)	Straße	*rushed*
u (long/short)	gut/und	*June*/*pull*
ü (long/short)	für/fünf	*'me'*/*'pin'* spoken with lips pouted
v	vier	*fine*
w	wo	*vain*
z	zehn	*fits*

Note about new spelling: new spelling rules were introduced in 1998 and are used in this course. Eszett, **ß**, is now used only after a long vowel, **Straße**, and **ss** after a short vowel, **dass**.

1 EINS

Guten Tag!

- **saying hello and goodbye**
- **introducing yourself**
- **socializing**

In Deutschland . . .

(in Germany), as **in Österreich** (in Austria) and **in der Schweiz** (in Switzerland), it is normal when greeting people to use the name of the person you are talking to and to shake hands. If you don't know the person's name, a simple greeting and handshake are sufficient. When you meet someone for the first time, you introduce yourself, usually giving your surname only, and shake hands, of course.

Saying hello . . .

1 Listen to these key phrases.

guten Morgen	good morning
guten Tag	good day/good afternoon
guten Abend	good evening

In all of the above, **guten** can be dropped for informal greetings:

Morgen   **Tag**   **Abend**

2 Listen to the members of staff greeting each other as they arrive for work at the Restaurant Franzl. Tick what time of day each of them arrives.

	Morning	Afternoon	Evening
a			
b			
c			
d			
e			

3 You may have noticed that some people use first names and some use the title **Herr** (for a man) or **Frau** (for a woman). Listen to the last conversations again and note down how often each is used.

First name ....   Herr ....   Frau ....

4 Listen to these key phrases.

wie geht es Ihnen?	how are you?
gut, danke, und Ihnen?	fine, thank you, and you?

5 When people know each other well, they often say **'wie geht's?'** Listen to the staff greeting each other at various times of day. How many of these people know each other well?

. . . and goodbye

6 Listen to these key phrases.

auf Wiedersehen	goodbye
Wiedersehen	'bye
tschüs	'bye
gute Nacht	goodnight, goodbye

7 Four diners are leaving the restaurant and saying goodbye to each other and the staff. Listen and number the speech bubbles below as you hear them.

8 Angelika is a receptionist at a large hotel. She speaks to five guests passing through the foyer. How many of them are leaving?

9 How would you greet these people at the times indicated?

11.30 a.m.	Barbara, a good friend
6.15 p.m.	Herr Scholz, restaurant manager
9.00 a.m.	Angelika Hoffmann, hotel receptionist
4.30 p.m.	Manfred, another good friend
7.30 p.m.	Rudi, a waiter

How would you ask Barbara and Herr Scholz how they are?

How would you say goodbye to Manfred and Rudi?

Introducing yourself . . .

1 Listen to these key phrases.

ich heiße . . .	I'm called . . .
mein Name ist . . .	my name is . . .
wie heißen Sie, bitte?	what's your name/what are you called, please?

2 At the restaurant, four people who have reserved tables give their names to Ulla, the receptionist. Number them 1 to 4 as you hear them and note down the time of day. You will notice that **Frau** is used as a courtesy title, whatever the age or marital status of the woman.

....	**Anna Blum**	....
....	**Heinrich Müller**	....
....	**Herr Brammerts**	....
....	**Barbara Goldmann**	....

3 One person walks past without speaking to Ulla, who asks politely who he is. Listen and write down the phrase he uses to give his name.

Ulla	**Guten Tag. Wie heißen Sie, bitte?**
Herr Altmann	.... **Altmann, Georg Altmann.**

4 Practise giving your own name, using the same phrase.

Auf Deutsch . . . (In German . . .)

bitte is used to oil the wheels of polite conversation. It can mean 'please', as in activity 3 above, but also, among other things, 'you're welcome', 'don't mention it' or 'here you are'. As you will see, **bitte** can also be teamed with other words.

. . . and socializing

5 Listen to these key phrases.

es freut mich/freut mich   pleased to meet you
wie bitte?   pardon?
und Sie?   and you?

6 Georg Altmann and Maria Schwarz meet for the first time. Listen to their conversation and fill the gaps below.

Maria	**Wie heißen ....?**
Georg	**Ich ....Georg Altmann. Und Sie?**
Maria	**Mein .... ist Schwarz, Maria Schwarz.**
Georg	**Wie bitte?**
Maria	**Maria Schwarz.**
Georg	**....................................., Frau Schwarz.**

7 Sometimes it's difficult to know if a name is a man's or a woman's. Here are some typical German names, several of which you have already heard. Listen to them and repeat. Check with the pronunciation guide on page 6 if you like.

Women:	**Ulla, Jutta, Inge, Kerstin, Liesl, Ulrike**
Men:	**Dieter, Rudi, Georg, Manfred, Hans, Udo**

8 Now listen to four conversations and tick the names that you hear.

Ulla	■	**Dieter**	■
Jutta	■	**Rudi**	■
Inge	■	**Georg**	■
Kerstin	■	**Manfred**	■
Liesl	■	**Hans**	■
Ulrike	■	**Udo**	■

Put it all together

1 Match the German phrases with their English equivalents.

a **Auf Wiedersehen**   How are you?
b **Wie heißen Sie?**   Pardon?
c **Tschüs**   Goodbye
d **Guten Tag**   Pleased to meet you
e **Wie bitte?**   What's your name?
f **Gute Nacht**   'bye
g **Freut mich**   Good night
h **Wie geht's?**   Good afternoon

2 What could these people be saying to each other?

3 Put these sentences into the correct order to make a conversation between two people meeting for the first time.

a **Mein Name ist Blum, Manfred Blum.**
b **Guten Abend. Wie heißen Sie, bitte?**
c **Guten Abend.**
d **Freut mich, Herr Blum.**
e **Ich heiße Ulrike Müller. Und Sie?**

❝ Now you're talking!

Imagine that you're having a drink in the hotel bar before lunch.

I There's a man standing at the bar.

◆ Greet him.
◇ **Guten Tag. Wie geht es Ihnen?**
◆ Say you're fine and ask how he is.
◇ **Gut, danke.**

2 A woman comes in and joins you.

◆ Greet her and introduce yourself.
◇ **Freut mich. Ich heiße Schneider, Anna Schneider.**
◆ You didn't catch her name. Say 'pardon?'
◇ **Frau Schneider, Anna Schneider.**
◆ Say you're pleased to meet her.

3 Someone else arrives.

◆ Greet him and ask his name.
◇ **Mein Name ist Offenbach.**
◆ Say you're pleased to meet him. Say who you are.

4 Your table is ready.

◆ Say goodbye to Frau Schneider and Herr Offenbach.

5 You've finished your meal.

◆ Say goodbye to Ulla Meyer, who is on duty, and wish her good night.

Quiz

1   When do you use **tschüs?**
2   How do you reply if someone says **Wie heißen Sie?**
3   What other way of introducing yourself have you learnt?
4   When do you say **Wie bitte?**
5   What is the German for 'pleased to meet you'?
6   It's midnight and you're leaving a party. What do you say?
7   How do you ask an acquaintance how they are?
8   The shop assistant says **Guten Morgen**. What time of day is it?

Now check whether you can . . .

- greet someone during the morning, afternoon and evening

- say goodbye

- say good night

- introduce yourself

- reply when people introduce themselves to you

- ask someone's name

- ask someone how they are

- reply when someone asks how you are

- ask for clarification if you don't catch what someone says

When you practise speaking, try to imitate the people you hear on the audio. Say the words and phrases out loud and repeat the same thing many times. Once you are confident about saying things, try to build up your speed.

2 Woher kommen Sie?

- saying where you're from
  - . . . and where your home town is
- saying what you do
- using the numbers 0 to 10

In Deutschland . . .

each **Land** (state) has a strong regional identity; Bavarians, for example, would describe themselves first and foremost as **Bayer**, speaking their own version of German, **bayerisch**. Austria (**Österreich**) and the German-speaking part of Switzerland (**die Schweiz**) also have their own regional characteristics in language, food and other aspects of daily life. In Southern Germany and Austria, for example, **Grüß Gott** is used as an all-purpose greeting and leave-taking.

Saying where you're from . . .

1 Listen to these key phrases.

woher kommen Sie?	where do you come from?
ich komme aus England	I come from England
sind Sie Engländer?	are you English?
ja, ich bin Engländer	yes, I'm English
nein, ich bin Waliserin	no, I'm Welsh
kommen Sie aus	do you come from Scotland
Schottland oder Irland?	or Ireland?

2 Brigitte, a courier for an international holiday company, is filling in forms with details of her latest group of tourists. Listen to their conversation. How many of the four people are English?

Auf Deutsch . . .

when talking about her nationality or job, a woman usually adds **-in** to whatever a man would say:

Engländer	**Engländerin**
Kanadier	**Kanadierin**
Österreicher	**Österreicherin**

There are some minor variations. For instance:

Schotte	**Schottin**	Scottish
Ire	**Irin**	Irish
Deutscher	**Deutsche**	German

3 Listen to eight more people from Brigitte's group and note down how many are men and how many women.

4 Listen again and see if you can work out what nationality they are. Many of the words sound very similar to English. They include:

Australier(in)   **Amerikaner(in)**   **Italiener(in)**   **Spanier(in)**

. . . and where your home town is

5 Listen to these key phrases.

wo wohnen Sie?	where do you live?
ich wohne in Wien	I live in Vienna
wo ist das?	where's that?
das ist in Österreich	it's in Austria
ich wohne in Padua in Italien	I live in Padua in Italy

6 Listen to four members of Brigitte's group telling her about themselves and complete the grid below.

Name	Town	Country
Peter Davies	Cardiff	Wales
Irene Fischer		
John McPhee		
Maeve Sullivan		

Auf Deutsch . . .

verbs have different endings according to which person they are referring to. The **ich** ending is usually **e**, and the **Sie** ending is almost always **en**:

Ich wohne in London.   **Wohnen Sie in Wien?**
Ich komme aus England.   **Kommen Sie aus Österreich?**

7 Listen to these short conversations and fill the gaps.

Georg	**Wo** .... **Sie, Frau Schwarz?**
Maria	**Ich** .... **in Wien in Österreich.**
Maria	.... **wohnen Sie?**
Anna	**Ich wohne** .... **Bozen in** .... **.**
Maria	**Und wo wohnen** .... **? Sind Sie Italiener?**
Carlos	**Nein, ich bin Spanier.** .... **wohne in Madrid.**

Saying what you do

1   Listen to these key phrases.

was sind Sie?	what are you/what do you do?
ich bin Sekretär(in)	I'm a secretary
ich bin Mechaniker(in)	I'm a mechanic
ich bin arbeitslos	I'm unemployed

Auf Deutsch . . .

when giving your nationality or job, 'a' is not used:

ich bin Hausfrau	I'm a housewife
ich bin Lehrer(in)	I'm a teacher

Have you noticed that all German nouns (words for things or people) are written with a capital letter?

2   Look at these jobs and see if you can identify the German equivalent of 'policewoman', 'student' and 'computer programmer'.

Sekretär	**Student**
Polizistin	**Hausfrau**
Programmierer	**Lehrerin**

How many of these words do you think refer to women? ....

3   Brigitte asks these members of her tour group what their occupations are. Listen and note them down in English.

Maeve Sullivan	....
Irene Fischer	....
Mark Smith	....
Elena Pastena	....
John McPhee	....
Peter Davies	....

Using the numbers 0 to 10

1   Look at the following handwritten numbers and note how 1 and 7 are written. Then listen to the numbers 0 to 10.

0   1   2   3   4   5   6   7   8   9   10
null eins zwei drei vier fünf sechs sieben acht neun zehn

2   Listen to the numbers being called for a game of **Lotto** (bingo) and circle those which appear on your card below.

1	3	8
2	6	10

Auf Deutsch . . .

as you may have noticed, **zwei** and **drei** sound very similar, so to prevent confusion German speakers often substitute **zwo** for **zwei** when giving important numbers.

3   Brigitte asks Irene, Mark and Peter what their telephone number is: **Was ist Ihre Telefonnummer?** Write the numbers in figures below.

Irene ....   Mark ....   Peter ....

4   Practise saying the following telephone numbers out loud, then check by listening to the cassette.

704568
591674
1253 6732
853197

5   Practise saying your own number, at home and/or at work.

Put it all together

1 Match the questions and the answers.

a **Sind Sie Amerikaner**   **Ich bin Hausfrau.**
   oder Kanadier?
b **Woher kommen Sie?**   **01982 46723**
c **Kommen Sie aus**   **Ich wohne in Stirling.**
   Schottland?
d **Wo wohnen Sie?**   **Aus Amerika.**
e **Was sind Sie?**   **Nein, ich komme aus Irland.**
f **Was ist Ihre Telefon-**   **Ich bin Kanadier.**
   nummer?

2 Read the descriptions given to Brigitte by three more tourists and complete the grid in English.

a **Ich heiße Helen Brownsmith. Ich bin Amerikanerin. Ich wohne in Washington und ich bin Lehrerin.**

b **Ich bin Österreicher. Ich heiße Georg Müller. Ich bin Programmier und ich wohne in Salzburg.**

c **Mein Name ist Andrew Hyde. Ich bin Schotte und ich wohne in Glasgow. Ich bin Polizist.**

Name	Nationality	Home town	Job
Helen Brownsmith	....	....	....
....	....	Salzburg	....
....	Scottish	....	....

3 Using the descriptions in activity 2 as a guide, write what Dieter and Juanita would say about themselves.

Dieter Hoffman
Austrian, from
Vienna
unemployed

Juanita Pueblos
Spanish, from
Madrid
student

Now you're talking!

1 When the tour reaches Dresden, the party splits
   up into small groups to visit the town. Helen gets
   talking to a customer in a shop. Answer as if you
   were Helen, giving information about yourself
   from the grid on the page opposite. The customer
   begins by asking 'Are you a foreigner?'

◇ **Sind Sie Ausländerin?**
◆ Say yes and tell her your nationality.
◇ **Wo wohnen Sie?**
◆ Say where you live.
◇ **Was sind Sie?**
◆ Say what you do.

2 David, another member of the group, has a similar conversation in a
   bar. Answer for him.

◇ **Herr Jones, Sind Sie**
   Engländer?
◆ You ....
◇ **Wo wohnen Sie in Wales?**
◆ You ....
◇ **Was sind Sie?**
◆ You ....
◇ **Und was ist Ihre**
   Telefonnummer?
◆ You ....

Name:	David Jones
Nationality:	Welsh
Home town:	Cardiff
Occupation:	Mechanic
Phone no.:	01643 9758

3 Georg initiates a conversation in a café. Ask the questions for him.

◆ Ask the person's name.
◇ **Ich heiße Ulrike Dietrich.**
◆ Ask where she lives.
◇ **Ich wohne in Kiel in Deutschland.**
◆ Ask what she does.
◇ **Ich bin Stewardess bei Lufthansa.**

Quiz

1 How does an American woman give her nationality?
2 How would you ask someone if they live in Leipzig?
3 How would you tell someone that you're from Chester?
4 How would you respond to the question **Sind Sie Italiener(in)?**
5 How does a woman student say what she does?
6 If a man says he is **Österreicher**, where is he from?
7 Fill in the missing numbers:
   drei, ..., **fünf**, **sechs**, ..., **acht**
8 Which is the odd one out?
   Lehrer, Schottin, Hausfrau, Sekretärin, Polizist

Now check whether you can . . .

■ say what nationality you are

■ say which country you are from

■ say which town you live in

■ say what work you do

■ ask others for this information

■ give your telephone number

It's a good idea at this stage to start organising your vocabulary learning. Write new words down in a book, put them on sticky labels in places where you can't fail to notice them, record them and get someone to test you on them. (It need not be a German speaker.) Make your vocabulary list relevant to you and your lifestyle. It's much easier to learn and retain words which are important to you.

Zwei Kaffee, bitte

- ● ordering a drink in a bar
  - . . . and in a café
- ● offering someone a drink
  - . . . and accepting or refusing

In Deutschland, in Österreich und in der Schweiz . . .

as in many other European countries, café life is popular. People relax for long periods over a cup of coffee; local and national newspapers are often available for customers to read. For people in a hurry, there is also the **Stehcafé** – literally, 'standing café' – where you can buy tea or coffee and perhaps a cake at the counter and stand to consume it at the nearest table. There are many varieties of coffee; the choice depends on the region. Most come with milk or cream, so you have to say how you want your coffee served.

Ordering a drink in a bar . . .

1   Listen to these key phrases.

bitte schön?	can I help you?
ein Bier, bitte	a beer, please
ein Glas Rotwein	a glass of red wine
ein Glas Weißwein	a glass of white wine
ein Mineralwasser	a mineral water
ich möchte eine Cola	I'd like a coke

2   Listen to people ordering these drinks and number them as you hear them.

.... **ein Mineralwasser**
.... **eine Cola**
.... **ein Glas Rotwein**
.... **ein Bier**

3   Some of the tourists in Brigitte's group go into a bar. Listen to Helen, Georg, Irene and Peter and note down in English what they order.

Helen ....
Georg ....
Irene ....
Peter ....

. . . and in a café

4 Listen to these key phrases.

eine Tasse Kaffee, bitte	a cup of coffee, please
ein Kännchen Tee	a pot of tea
eine Schokolade	a drinking chocolate
mit Sahne	with cream
ohne Milch	without milk
zwei Tassen Tee	two cups of tea
sonst noch etwas?	anything else?

5 Now listen to six people ordering drinks and tick the boxes to show what they want.

	a	b	c	d	e	f
ein Kännchen Tee	■	■	■	■	■	■
eine Tasse Tee	■	■	■	■	■	■
ein Kännchen Kaffee	■	■	■	■	■	■
eine Tasse Kaffee	■	■	■	■	■	■
mit Milch	■	■	■	■	■	■
ohne Milch	■	■	■	■	■	■
mit Sahne	■	■	■	■	■	■
eine Schokolade	■	■	■	■	■	■

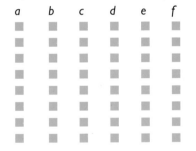

Auf Deutsch . . .

when ordering drinks, most words don't change in the plural: **ein Bier, zwei Bier; ein Glas Rotwein, drei Glas Rotwein**. One that does change is **Tasse: eine Tasse Tee, zwei Tassen Tee**. German plurals are formed in a variety of ways, so it is best to learn the ones you need as you meet them.

6 How would you ask for the following?

- a pot of tea with milk
- a cup of tea without milk
- a pot of coffee
- two cups of coffee with cream

Offering someone a drink . . .

1 Listen to these key phrases.

was möchten Sie?	what would you like?
möchten Sie einen Kaffee?	would you like a coffee?
und für Sie?	and for you?
noch einen Kaffee?	another coffee?

2 Listen to the conversation and fill the gaps below.

Georg **Maria, was** .... **Sie?**
Maria **Oh, ein** .... **Wein, bitte.**
Georg **Ein Glas** ....?
Maria **Nein,** ....
Georg **Und** .... **Sie, Franz?** .... **einen Kaffee?**

Auf Deutsch . . .

nouns divide into three categories or 'genders' – masculine, feminine and neuter – and this affects words used with them, like 'a' and 'the'. They're also affected by the way the noun is used in the sentence. When you ask for or offer something, the word for 'a' is as follows:

möchten Sie einen Kaffee? – masculine (m.)
möchten Sie eine Tasse Tee? – feminine (f.)
möchten Sie ein Bier? – neuter (n.)

3 How would you offer someone these drinks?

- a coffee
- a glass of beer
- a cup of tea with milk
- another coffee
- a coke

. . . and accepting or refusing

4 Listen to these key phrases.

gern	I'd love one
ja, danke	yes, thank you
danke schön	thank you very much
nichts für mich, danke	nothing for me, thank you
nein, danke	no, thank you
prost!	cheers!

5 Georg offers several people drinks. Listen and tick the ones who accept.

Barbara   *Manfred*

Irene   *Angelika*

Franz

Prost!

6 Listen to the conversation in activity 5 again and decide which of the bills is Georg's.

a

> **1 Bier**
> **1 Glas Rotwein**
> **2 Kaffee**

c

> **1 Kaffee**
> **1 Bier**
> **1 Glas Rotwein**

b

> **1 Bier**
> **2 Glas Rotwein**
> **1 Tasse Tee**

d

> **2 Glas Rotwein**
> **2 Kaffee**

7 And now decide what to say when . . .

- you raise your glass to your friends
- you thank someone very much for their offer

Put it all together

I Irene is at the bar, ordering three glasses of white wine and a beer. The man next to her is ordering three beers, a coke and a mineral water. Write down what each will say in German.

Irene ....

Mann ....

2 Which is the right phrase for each situation?

I You refuse the offer of a coffee.
   a **Prost!**   *b* **Nein, danke.**
   c **Ohne Sahne.**

2 You offer someone a drink.
   a **Bitte schön?**   *b* **Sonst noch etwas?**
   c **Was möchten Sie?**

3 You would like your coffee with milk.
   a **Mit Milch.**   *b* **Ohne Milch.**
   c **Mit Sahne.**

4 You'd love to accept a glass of red wine.
   a **Und für Sie?**   *b* **Für mich nichts.**
   c **Gern.**

3 Complete this conversation with the waiter (**Ober**) in a restaurant, using the words in the box.

Ober	**Guten Abend. Bitte schön?**
Jutta	**Ich .... Kaffee, bitte.**
	Und für ...., Liesl?
Liesl	**Für .... ein Bier.**
Jutta	**Und Sie, Manfred?**
Manfred	**Für mich ...., ...**
Jutta	**Gut. Ein Bier und einen Kaffee,**
	....
Ober	**Sonst noch etwas?**
Jutta	**................, danke.**

möchte
nein
mich
bitte
Sie
danke
nichts
einen

Now you're talking!

1   You meet two colleagues in a café. One of them offers you a drink.

◇ **Möchten Sie einen Kaffee?**
◆ Say yes, you'd love one.
◇ **Mit oder ohne Sahne?**
◆ Say with cream, please.

Now it's your turn to order.
◆ Ask Franz what he would like.
◇ **Ein Mineralwasser, bitte.**
◆ Ask Irene if she'd like another coffee.
◇ **Ja, danke.**
◆ Order a mineral water, a cup of coffee and a pot of tea.

2   You are out with a large group of friends and have noted down what they want to drink. The waitress comes over.

◇ **Bitte schön.**
◆ Ask for a cup of tea with milk and two pots of coffee.

Later, a waiter comes up to you.
◇ **Bitte schön.**
◆ Order a glass of white wine, two glasses of coke and four beers.

3   Now take part in a conversation in a bar. The waiter approaches.

◇ **Bitte schön?**
◆ Ask your companion if she would like a beer.
◇ **Ja, gern.**
◆ You are joined by Dieter and Kerstin. Offer Dieter a drink.
◇ **Für mich ein Glas Bier.**
◆ And Kerstin?
◇ **Für mich ein Glas Rotwein.**
◆ Give the waiter the order, plus a glass of white wine for you.
◇ **Sonst noch etwas?**
◆ Say no thank you.
◆ The drinks arrive. Thank the waiter, then say cheers!

Quiz

1 If you order **Kaffee mit Milch**, will it be white or black?
2 **Rotwein**, **Weißwein** – which is the red wine?
3 You offer someone a drink and they say **gern**. Are they accepting or refusing?
4 **Noch drei Bier** – what have you ordered?
5 What does the waiter want to know if he says **Sonst noch etwas?**
6 Name two alcoholic drinks in German.
7 Which of these drinks could you have **mit Sahne**?
   Cola, Kaffee, Tee
8 You want a pot of tea. Do you ask for **eine Tasse** or **ein Kännchen**?

Now check whether you can . . .

■ order a drink

■ offer someone a drink

■ accept when someone offers you a drink

   . . . or refuse politely

■ say how you want your drink

■ order more drinks

■ say cheers!

When you meet a word for the first time, it's a good idea to check in the glossary whether it's masculine, feminine or neuter. Nouns are listed there with the word for 'the', which shows which category they belong to: **der Kaffee**, (m.); **die Schokolade**, (f.); **das Bier**, (n.). You'll find it quite easy to remember if you learn each word together with **der**, **die** or **das** as you go along.

4 VIER

Darf ich vorstellen?

- introducing someone
- talking about family
- asking and giving someone's age
- using the numbers up to 100

In Deutschland, in Österreich und in der Schweiz . . .

families still gather at traditional times, especially to celebrate Christmas and New Year. Many regions have their own distinctive ways of celebrating these and other festivals, and the predominantly Catholic southern areas have extra public holidays associated with saints' days. Despite changing work patterns, many people stay in their home region and thus maintain close family ties.

Introducing someone

1 Listen to these key phrases.

darf ich vorstellen?	may I introduce (you)?
das ist mein Mann	this is my husband
das ist meine Frau	this is my wife
das sind meine Freunde	these are my friends
freut mich	pleased to meet you
ebenfalls	likewise ('pleased to meet you too')

Auf Deutsch . . .

Frau and **Herr**, as you will remember, mean 'Mrs' and 'Mr'. **Frau** has additional meanings: **meine Frau** means 'my wife' and **eine Frau** means 'a woman'. The word for 'man' and 'husband', however, is **Mann**, not **Herr**.

Notice that 'my' has different forms depending on the noun it's used with: **mein Mann** (m.), but **meine Frau** (f.).

2 Some members of the tour group are getting to know each other. Listen and fill the gaps in their conversations.

a *Irene Fischer*   **Darf ich** ....**? Das** .... **mein Mann, Karl Fischer.**

    Joachim Schneider   **Freut mich. Mein Name ist Joachim Schneider.**

b *Joachim Schneider*   .... **ich vorstellen? Das** .... **meine Freunde, Bob und Joan Butler.**

    Irene Fischer   **Es freut mich, Herr Butler, Frau Butler.**

    Bob Butler   ....

3 Liesl and Hans are a married couple. How would each introduce the other?

    Liesl   **Darf ich vorstellen?** ....

    Hans   ....

Talking about family

1 Listen to these key phrases.

sind Sie verheiratet?   are you married?
ja, ich bin verheiratet   yes, I'm married
nein, ich bin nicht verheiratet   no, I'm not married

2 Listen to Joachim Förster talking to Brigitte and her colleagues, Herr Koch and Frau Schwarz. Who is married?

3 Listen to these key phrases.

haben Sie Kinder?   have you any children?
ich habe keine Kinder   I don't have children
ja, ich habe . . .   yes, I have . . .
. . . eine Tochter/zwei Töchter   . . . a daughter/two daughters
. . . einen Sohn/drei Söhne   . . . a son/three sons

4 Listen to Brigitte asking for information and complete the form.

NAME	FAMILIENSTAND	KINDER
Irene Fischer	verheiratet	....
Joachim Schneider	....	....
Georg Müller	....	....

Asking and giving someone's age

1   Listen to these key phrases.

wie alt sind Sie?	how old are you?
ich bin vierundzwanzig Jahre alt	I'm 24 years old
wie alt ist er? er ist fünfzehn	how old is he? he's 15
mein Sohn ist sechzehn	my son is 16
wie alt ist sie? sie ist elf	how old is she? she's 11
meine Tochter ist zwölf	my daughter is 12

2   Now listen to all the numbers from 11 to 19. You'll recognize 3 to 9 in the numbers 13 to 19.

elf, zwölf, dreizehn, vierzehn, fünfzehn,   11, 12, 13, 14, 15,
sechzehn, siebzehn, achtzehn, neunzehn   16, 17, 18, 19

3   Listen and note down the ages of these children.

Fritz ....   Maria ....   Liesl ....   Jutta ....

4   How would Herr Altmann state his children's ages? Write the numbers out in words.

> ★★★ **Campingplatz am Rheinufer**
>
> **Familienname:**   Altmann
> **Kinder:**   Manfred 19; Angelika 16; Daniel 11

Mein Sohn Manfred ....
Meine ....
....

Using the numbers up to 100

1 Listen to the numbers 20 to 25.

20 **zwanzig**   23 **dreiundzwanzig**
21 **einundzwanzig**   24 **vierundzwanzig**
22 **zweiundzwanzig**   25 **fünfundzwanzig**

2 Before you listen to 26 to 29, try to fill the gaps.

26 ....**undzwanzig**   28 ....**undzwanzig**
27 **siebenund**...........   29 **neun**...........

In German, the numbers above 20 are written and spoken in the
reverse order to English: **einundzwanzig** – 'one and twenty',
zweiundzwanzig – 'two and twenty', and so on.

3 Now listen to these larger numbers.

30 **dreißig**   60 **sechzig**   90 **neunzig**
40 **vierzig**   70 **siebzig**   100 **hundert**
50 **fünfzig**   80 **achtzig**

Hundert on its own means 'a hundred' or 'one hundred'.

4 The pattern you saw in 21 to 29 is repeated in numbers up to 100.
Complete the numbers 41 to 49.

41 **einundvierzig**   44 **vierundvierzig**   47 **sieben**.........**vierzig**
42 **zweiundvierzig**   45 ....**undvierzig**   48 **achtundvierzig**
43 ....**undvierzig**   46 **sechsund**.........   49 ....

5 Listen to people talking about their families and circle the number you
hear in each of these pairs.

a 23   32   d 70   17
b 15   50   e 59   49
c 46   64

Put it all together

I The Bradshaws are planning a house swap with Familie Friedmann.
Read what Dieter writes about his family.

*Darf ich vorstellen? Mein Name ist Dieter Friedmann. Ich bin
verheiratet und habe einen Sohn und eine Tochter. Ich bin vierundvierzig
Jahre alt, meine Frau Kerstin ist achtunddreißig. Mein Sohn Helmut
ist fünfzehn und meine Tochter Susanna ist elf.*

Write an introduction from the Bradshaws. Here is the information
about them.

Jack aged 48
Mary aged 47
Frank aged 26
Julia aged 24

2 Put these sentences into
the correct order to make a conversation between Joachim Schneider
and Heinz Wolf.

a **Wie alt ist Grete?**
b **Ja, meine Frau heißt Julia. Und Sie?**
c **Sie ist zwölf.**
d **Sind Sie verheiratet, Herr Wolf?**
e **Ja, ich habe eine Tochter, Grete.**
f **Nein, ich bin nicht verheiratet. Haben Sie Kinder?**

3 Match the family to the house.

Familie
Förster
zweiundfünfzig

Familie
Lindemann
neunundvierzig

Familie
Martens
einundfünfzig

Familie
Schröder
achtundvierzig

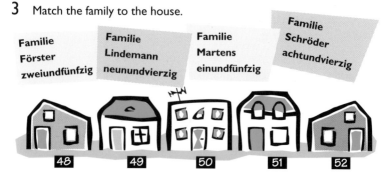

48   49   50   51   52

Now you're talking!

Take the part of Robert Blythe, who is talking to a fellow guest in the hotel lounge.

I Your new acquaintance asks about you and your family. Read the questions and prepare your answers before speaking.

Clare   Jenny   Robert

Wie heißen Sie? ....
Sind Sie verheiratet? ....
Und haben Sie Kinder? ....
Haben Sie einen Sohn? ....
Wie alt ist Jenny? ....

2 Two more people join you. Your new acquaintance introduces them.

◇ **Darf ich vorstellen? Das sind meine Freunde, Stephanie und Georg Krumm . . . Herr Blythe.**
◇ **Freut mich, Herr Blythe.**
◆ Respond to Frau Krumm's greeting.

Just then, your wife arrives.
◆ Introduce her to Mr and Mrs Krumm.
◇ **Freut mich, Frau Blythe.**

3 Ask Mrs Krumm these questions and listen to her replies:

◆ has she any children?
◆ how old is her son?

Quiz

1   How would a woman introduce her husband?
2   Someone says **Freut mich**. What might you reply?
3   If someone says **Ich habe keine Kinder**, what are they telling you?
4   How do you say how old you are in German?
5   If someone says **Ich bin achtzehn Jahre alt**, are they 8, 18 or 80?
6   When referring to a daughter, would you say **sie** or **er**?
7   Does the word **verheiratet** describe a married or a single person?
8   How does someone say that they have three sons?

Now check whether you can . . .

- introduce someone – male or female

- give your age

- say how old someone else is

- ask other people for this information

- say whether you are married

- say whether you have any children

- say how many sons and daughters you have

- use the numbers 11 to 100

At this early stage in your language learning, the secret is to *keep it simple*. You can pick up the words of a question to form your answer: **Sind Sie verheiratet?** can help you to answer **Ja, ich bin verheiratet**. And **Nein, ich bin nicht verheiratet** will cover separated, divorced and widowed, as well as single. You will be surprised how much you can convey with a few words.

Kontrollpunkt 1

1 Choose the appropriate expression for each situation.

Guten Abend!   **Prost!**   **Aus England.**   **Nein, danke.**
Ja, einen Sohn.   **Sind Sie verheiratet?**   **Gute Nacht.**

a Answering **Haben Sie Kinder?** ....
b Saying 'cheers'. ....
c Refusing an offer of a drink. ....
d Greeting someone at 7 p.m. ....
e Asking if someone is married. ....
f Saying good night/goodbye. ....
g Answering **Woher kommen Sie?** ....

2 Listen to Detlev and Sylvia as they get to know each other at a party, and fill in the information you learn in the grid below.

Name	Nationality	Occupation	Family
Detlev	....	....	....
Sylvia	....	....	....

3 Brigitte has filled in a form for two of her tourists, but she was tired and made a number of errors. Listen and correct the form.

Name	Nationalität	Beruf	Alter	Familie
Miller, Margaret	Kanadierin	Polizistin	35	einen Sohn
Carter, Steven	Engländer	Lehrer	42	keine Kinder

4 Brigitte and Joachim are joined for a drink by Irene and Georg. Listen and note in English what each one has.

Brigitte ....   Irene   ....
Georg ....   Joachim ....

5 *a* Say the following numbers aloud and then check by listening to the audio.

71   12   89   45   54

b Brigitte is giving Martha her phone number. Listen and tick the correct number below.

178263   168263   178253

6 Rudi, the waiter, is applying for a job in England and would like help in filling in his application form. What questions would you need to ask him in order to find out the missing information?

Name:	.............................*a*.............................
Address:	Rudolfstraße 14, DRESDEN
Tel. No:	065 435 98
Age:	.............................*b*.............................
Marital status:	.............................*c*.............................
Nationality:	German
Occupation:	.............................*d*.............................

a ....
b ....
c ....
d ....

7 You're in a café, ordering for yourself and some friends. Barbara wants a cup of coffee; Carla wants a lemonade; Michael wants a beer; Rolf wants a glass of red wine and you want a glass of white wine. What will you say to the waiter when he comes up and asks for your order? Listen to the audio to see if you're right.

8 A neighbour's son receives a letter from a new German penfriend. Some words, or parts of words, are unreadable because the letter got wet. Help him to reconstruct it and answer his questions below. (Check the unfamiliar words in the glossary after you have made a guess at what they mean.)

> Stuttgart
> 1. August
>
> Lieber Paul,
>
>   ich heiße Tobias und wohne in Deutschland, in Stuttgart. Ich bin 14 Jahre alt. Mein Vater ist Programmierer und meine Mutter ist Sekretärin bei Woolworths. Ich habe eine Schwester, Susi, und einen Bruder, Jochen. Susi ist 19 und ist Studentin an der Universität Marburg. Jochen ist 22 und ist schon verheiratet. Seine Frau kommt aus Italien. Er ist arbeitslos und sie ist Lehrerin.

Missing words: ....
....
....

a What do Tobias' brother and sister do?
....

b What do Tobias' father and mother do?
....

c How old is Tobias?
....

d What nationality is Jochen's wife?
....

9 Can you find the German words for the following, hidden in the grid? They are written upwards or downwards, left to right or right to left. (Umlauts have been omitted and ß is written as ss.)

a   Good morning ....

b   Goodbye (formal) ....

c   Goodbye (informal) ....

d   My name is ....

e   Pleased to meet you ....

f   Hello (in S. Germany/Austria) ....

g   Thank you ....

h   I am ....

i   Good evening ....

j   How are you? (formal) ....

G	U	T	E	N	M	O	R	G	E	N	A
R	A	N	K	S	E	I	T	U	B	E	U
W	L	T	N	C	I	H	E	T	I	N	F
K	N	E	A	H	N	A	D	E	S	H	W
O	I	S	D	A	R	N	E	N	H	I	I
R	K	E	H	L	P	O	K	A	C	S	E
T	W	I	S	T	M	R	A	B	U	E	D
T	R	S	U	H	C	S	T	E	T	T	E
O	H	C	I	R	N	I	G	N	L	H	R
G	C	A	C	H	E	M	E	D	I	E	S
S	S	R	H	A	S	T	D	E	M	G	E
S	U	M	B	S	E	E	G	S	K	E	H
U	H	C	I	M	T	U	E	R	F	I	E
R	B	O	N	F	I	R	U	A	C	W	N
G	T	S	I	E	M	A	N	N	I	E	M

Wo ist die Bank?

FÜNF

- enquiring about places in town
  - . . . and understanding where they are
- following simple directions
- asking for help with understanding

In Deutschland, in Österreich und in der Schweiz . . .

the market square (**Marktplatz**), with the town hall (**Rathaus**) and often a fountain (**Brunnen**), is still the heart of many small towns. Most modern cities retain their old town centre (**Altstadt**) with its historic buildings. Every town has an information office, which may be called **Verkehrsamt**, **Verkehrsverein** or **Verkehrsbüro**. It is instantly recognised by the international symbol **i** for information (**Auskunft**).

Enquiring about places in town . . .

1 Listen to these key phrases.

entschuldigen Sie	excuse me
wo ist die Bank?	where's the bank?
wo ist der Bahnhof?	where's the station?
ist das die Post?	is that the post office?
ist das weit von hier?	is it far from here?

2 Five tourists stop Rudi on the street to ask about these places. Listen and number them in the order you hear them.

die Post

die Bank

das Rathaus

der Marktplatz

der Bahnhof

3 Now listen to more tourists asking about places and fill the blanks in the sentences below. You will hear the words for 'the cathedral' and 'the shopping centre'; you can check in the glossary if you are not sure which is which.

a **Entschuldigen Sie, ... der Bahnhof, bitte?**
b **Wo ist der Dom? Ist das .... von hier?**
c **Wo ist ...., bitte?**
d **........................... Sie, ist das das Verkehrs ....?**
e **Ist das Einkaufszentrum weit ....?**

. . . and understanding where they are

4 Listen to these key phrases.

wir sind hier	we are here
die Post ist links	the post office is on the left
die Bank ist rechts	the bank is on the right
da drüben	over there
geradeaus	straight on
es ist fünf Minuten zu Fuß	it's five minutes on foot

5 Brigitte is showing Irene where places are on a plan of Neustadt, including **die Apotheke** (the chemist's). Listen and note down the places mentioned. Then listen again and mark each place R (right), L (left), S (straight on) or O (over there).

a ....   d ....

b ....   e ....

c ....

6 Read the information below and label the places numbered 1 to 5 on the map.

**Das Verkehrsamt ist links.
Die Apotheke ist hier rechts
und das Rathaus ist da drüben
rechts. Der Dom ist geradeaus
am Marktplatz und der Bahnhof
ist auch geradeaus – fünf
Minuten zu Fuß.**

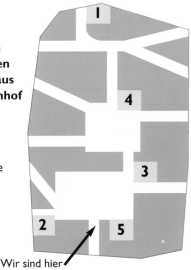

Wir sind hier

7 How would you ask where these places are?

- the station
- the tourist office
- the cathedral

Following simple directions

1 Listen to these key phrases.

gehen Sie . . .	go . . .
. . . um die Ecke	. . . round the corner
. . . hier links	. . . left here
nehmen Sie . . .	take . . .
. . . die erste Straße rechts	. . . the first road on the right
. . . die zweite Straße links	. . . the second road on the left
das ist neben dem Museum	it's next to the museum
gegenüber dem Bahnhof	opposite the station
nicht weit von der Post	not far from the post office

2 A Neustadt tourist office employee is answering tourists' questions.
As you listen, tick the correct instructions below, then rewrite the
incorrect ones.

a **Der Dom? Gehen Sie geradeaus und dann rechts.**
b **Das Verkehrsamt ist da drüben, neben der Bank.**
c **Der Bahnhof ist hier links.**
d **Das Einkaufszentrum ist rechts um die Ecke.**
e **Der Dom ist gegenüber der Bank.**
f **Nehmen Sie die zweite Straße rechts und die Apotheke
ist neben der Post.**

Auf Deutsch . . .

after some locating words, including **gegenüber**, **neben** and **von**:
- **der** and **das** change to **dem**: **gegenüber dem Bahnhof**
- **die** changes to **der**: **von der Post**

3 Complete these directions.

a **Das Museum ist neben** .... **Bahnhof.**
b **Der Parkplatz ist nicht weit von** .... **Bank.**
c **Die Post ist gegenüber** .... **Einkaufszentrum.**
d **Der Dom ist neben** .... **Marktplatz.**

Asking for help with understanding

I Listen to these key phrases.

bitte wiederholen Sie   please repeat that
sprechen Sie langsamer, bitte please speak more slowly
ich verstehe nicht   I don't understand
ich bin fremd hier   I'm a stranger here

Auf Deutsch . . .

as in other languages, words are often used which don't add essential information to the sentence. Listen out in this unit for **dann**, **vielleicht** and **auch**, and see if you can work out what they mean. The answers are given later.

2 Listen to Rudi helping some tourists on his way to work. Note down in English the place each one is looking for. Listen a second time and note (also in English) what problem each one has.

	Place	Problem
Irene		
Anna		
Maria		
Jutta		

3 Which of the phrases above would you use in the following situations? (There may be more than one possible answer, or you could use a combination of phrases.)

a You ask someone for information; they think you are a fluent speaker and reply very quickly.
b You don't know the town and ask a passer-by for help.
c Someone gives you directions, but you can't take it all in at once.
d Someone uses a lot of words which are new to you.

Put it all together

1 How would you ask where these places are?

a ....

b ....

c ....

d ....

e ....

f ....

2 Follow the directions below on the map and write down where you get to.

a **Gehen Sie geradeaus, nehmen Sie die zweite Straße links. Das ist da links.**

b **Das ist da drüben rechts.**

c **Gehen Sie hier rechts um die Ecke. Das ist neben der Post.**

d **Gehen Sie geradeaus.**

3 Look at the map again and write down the directions for

a the museum

   ....

b the bank

   ....

Now you're talking!

1   Before leaving your hotel to look round Neustadt, you ask the receptionist for some information.

- ◆ Greet her and ask where the cathedral is.
- ◇ **Der Dom? Der Dom ist neben dem Rathaus.**
- ◆ Ask if it's far.
- ◇ **Nein, zehn Minuten zu Fuß.**
- ◆ Now ask where the bank is.
- ◇ **Gegenüber dem Rathaus.**
- ◆ Thank her and say goodbye.

2   Later you ask a man outside the cathedral for help.

- ◆ Ask him where the shopping centre is.
- ◇ **Das ist nicht weit – geradeaus, die zweite Straße rechts und da ist es.**
- ◆ Ask him to repeat what he said.
- ◇ **Das ist nicht weit – immer geradeaus, die zweite Straße rechts und da ist es.**
- ◆ Say you don't understand. Ask him to speak more slowly.

3   After a break in a café, you decide to go to the tourist office, so you stop a passer-by.

- ◆ Say excuse me and explain that you're a stranger to the town.
- ◇ **Ja?**
- ◆ Ask where the tourist office is.
- ◇ **Gehen Sie rechts um die Ecke.**
- ◆ Say thank you and goodbye.

4   Outside the tourist office, a stranger asks you where the cathedral is. You've been there, so you can give directions. Say.

- ◆ Go straight ahead.
- ◆ Take the first on the right.
- ◆ The cathedral is on the left, next to the town hall.

Quiz

1   If someone says **Das Einkaufszentrum ist da drüben**, what are
    they telling you?
2   You want to find a chemist's. Which of these phrases do you use?
    Wo ist die Post/die Apotheke/der Bahnhof?
3   How do you tell someone that you don't understand?
4   What directions are you given here? **Gehen Sie geradeaus.**
5   And here? **Nehmen Sie die zweite Straße links.**
6   When would you say **Sprechen Sie langsamer, bitte?**
7   **neben**, **gegenüber**, **nicht weit von** – which means 'next to'?
8   **Verkehrsverein**, **Verkehrsamt** – what other word do you know
    for 'tourist information office'?

Now check whether you can . . .

   ▪ remember the names of places in town

   ▪ ask where they are

   ▪ understand simple directions

   ▪ explain that you are a stranger

   ▪ say that you cannot understand

   ▪ ask people to repeat information

   ▪ ask people to speak more slowly

In several conversations you will have noticed some extra words
which occur naturally but don't add essential information: **dann**
means 'then', **vielleicht** 'perhaps', **auch** 'also'. You probably
understood them as you heard them. These 'fillers' help conversation
to flow. Why not try using some yourself?

6

SECHS

Haben Sie Orangen?

- asking for what you want

  . . . and understanding the assistant

- buying the quantity you want

- dealing with money

In Deutschland, in Österreich und in der Schweiz . . .

although there are large supermarkets and department stores, more shopping is done in small specialist shops than in Britain. The market is still an important place for buying fresh produce. Small shops and cafés open early to catch people on their way to work, and bread shops in the suburbs of cities and in small towns and villages supply fresh rolls for breakfast.

Asking for what you want . . .

1 Listen to these key phrases.

haben Sie Orangen?	have you any oranges?
was kostet eine Ananas?	how much is a pineapple?
was kosten die Bananen?	how much are the bananas?
das ist alles	that's everything

2 Listen to three people shopping. Note in English what they want.

a ....

b ....

c ....

Auf Deutsch . . .

to ask the price of one item, you use **kostet** (costs): **es kostet vier Euro**; for more than one item, you use **kosten** (cost): **was kosten die Orangen?** For more on verb patterns like these, see page 120.

3 Barbara is at the market, buying fruit for a picnic. Listen and complete her conversation with the stallholder (**Verkäufer**).

Verkäufer	**Bitte schön?**
Barbara	**Was .... die Bananen?**
Verkäufer	**Vier Bananen kosten einen Euro fünfzig (€ 1,50).**
Barbara	**Und .... Sie Orangen?**
Verkäufer	**Ja, hier. Eine Orange .... dreißig Cent (Ct. 30).**
Barbara	**Ich möchte sechs.**
Verkäufer	**Sonst noch etwas?**
Barbara	**Ja, was .... eine Ananas?**
Verkäufer	**Zwei Euro fünfzig (€ 2,50).**
Barbara	**Gut. Vier Bananen, sechs Orangen und eine Ananas, bitte.**

. . . and understanding the assistant

4 Listen to these key phrases.

kann ich Ihnen helfen?	can I help you?
die hier?	these here?
. . . das Stück	. . . each
. . . das Kilo	. . . a kilo

5 Listen as Barbara does some more shopping. First she buys tomatoes (**Tomaten**) and grapes (**Trauben**), then she goes to the baker's for fresh rolls (**Brötchen**). Number the phrases above as you hear them.

Auf Deutsch . . .

the currency in Germany is the euro (**Euro**). **1 Euro = 100 Cent**. Note that there is no plural -s for Euro and Cent when used with numbers. You'll hear different ways in which euro amounts are expressed: € 2,40 (two euros forty cents) may be either **zwei Euro vierzig** or simply **zwei vierzig**. Note that a comma is used for the decimal point.

6 Now listen to Barbara's conversations again and write the prices in figures. Can you work out her total bill?

a *Verkäufer* **Guten Tag. Kann ich Ihnen helfen?**
   Barbara **Ja, ich möchte sechs Tomaten, bitte.**
   Verkäufer **Sechs Tomaten kosten € ....**
   Sonst noch etwas?
   Barbara **Ja, und die Trauben.**
   Verkäufer **Die hier? Gut. Sie kosten € .... das Kilo.**
   Barbara **Danke.**

b *Verkäuferin* **Guten Tag.**
   Barbara **Guten Tag. Ich möchte Brötchen, bitte.**
   Was kosten sie?
   Verkäuferin **.................. Cent das Stück.**
   Barbara **Ich möchte zehn, bitte.**

Buying the quantity you want

1   Listen to these words for saying precisely how much you want.

1 kg	ein Kilo	1 l	ein Liter
½ kg	ein halbes Kilo	½ l	ein halber Liter
250 g	250 Gramm	¼ l	ein Viertelliter
100 g	100 Gramm		

2   Listen to Dieter checking his shopping list and write down the quantity you hear beside each item.

a   .... **Trauben**   c   .... **Rotwein**
b   .... **Milch**   d   .... **Tomaten**

Auf Deutsch . . .

there is no word for 'of' with quantities and containers:
    ein Kilo Trauben   a kilo of grapes
    ein Glas Bier   a glass of beer

3   Listen to people asking for the following things and number them as you hear them.

eine Dose Tomaten   a can of tomatoes
ein Päckchen Kekse   a packet of biscuits
eine Flasche Orangensaft   a bottle of orange juice
eine Packung Apfelsaft   a carton of apple juice

4   Now listen and complete Gerlinde's shopping list.

1 .... **Orangensaft**
½ kg ....
1 l ....
1 .... **Kaffee**
6 ....
1 .... **Cola**
1 **Packung**
.... **Tee**

Dealing with money

1 Listen to these key phrases.

ich möchte diesen Reisescheck einlösen	I'd like to cash this traveller's cheque
wo kann ich Geld wechseln?	where can I change money?
kann ich mit Kreditkarte bezahlen?	can I pay by credit card?

2 Listen to three short conversations and note down in English what each person wants to do.

Manfred ....

Georg ....

Maria ....

Auf Deutsch . . .

when saying what you can do or would like to do, the verb expressing this goes to the end:

Wo kann ich Geld wechseln?
literally: 'Where can I money to change?'
Ich möchte mit Kreditkarte bezahlen.
literally: 'I'd like by credit card to pay.'

3 Complete these **kann** and **möchte** sentences, using the most suitable verb from the key phrases above.

a **Kann ich hier Geld** ....?

b **Wo kann ich diesen Reisescheck** ....?

c **Ich möchte meine Reiseschecks** ....

Put it all together

1 Tick the box(es) in the grid below to indicate the quantities or containers in which you would buy the items on the left. The first one has been done for you.

	250 g	Flasche	Dose	Päckchen	I Liter
Tee	✔			✔	
Trauben					
Apfelsaft					
Kekse					
Wein					
Cola					

2 To prepare for your shopping trip, put your list into German.

1 bottle of orange juice
1 litre of red wine
½ kilo of tomatoes
4 bananas
1 can of tomatoes
1 packet of biscuits
6 rolls

3 Match the two halves of the sentences.

a **Was kosten**   **Kreditkarte bezahlen?**
b **Ich möchte diesen**   **helfen?**
c **Wo kann ich**   **eine Ananas?**
d **Kann ich Ihnen**   **Reisescheck einlösen.**
e **Was kostet**   **Geld wechseln?**
f **Kann ich mit**   **die Orangen?**

"Now you're talking!

You have a busy morning's shopping ahead of you!

1 At the market: **Auf dem Markt**

The woman at the fruit stall greets you.

◇ **Tag. Kann ich Ihnen helfen?**
◆ Greet the stallholder and ask for 250 grammes of grapes and a kilo of bananas.
◇ **Sonst noch etwas?**
◆ You want half a kilo of tomatoes.
◇ **Gut. Und sonst noch etwas?**
◆ Say no, that's all, and thank the stallholder.

2 At the grocer's: **Im Lebensmittelgeschäft**

◆ Ask for six bread rolls.
◇ **Sonst noch etwas?**
◆ Ask how much a packet of biscuits costs.
◇ **€ 1,50 das Päckchen.**
◆ Say you'd like a packet and a bottle of red wine.
◇ **Sonst noch etwas?**
◆ Say yes, you'd like a litre of apple juice.
◇ **Gut. € 10,80 bitte.**

3 You go to the bank for more money.

◆ Greet the cashier and say you'd like to change some money.
◆ When he tells you the amount in euros, say thank you and goodbye.

Quiz

1 Would you use **Was kostet . . . ?** or **Was kosten . . . ?** to ask the price of: *a* **fünf Brötchen**, *b* **eine Ananas**, *c* **eine Dose Cola**?
2 At the market, how would you ask if they have any tomatoes?
3 How many **Cent** are there in a **Euro**?
4 If **ein Schinkenbrötchen** is a ham roll, how would you ask for a tomato roll?
5 Which word means 'to cash': **wechseln** or **einlösen**?
6 How much wine would you get in a **Viertelliterglas**?
7 If you asked for **zehn Orangen**, what would you expect to get?
8 Would **Apfelsaft** be most likely to come in a **Dose**, a **Packung** or a **Päckchen**?

Now check whether you can . . .

■ ask how much something costs

■ understand the answer

■ say that you'd like something

■ ask for the quantity you want

■ specify the container something comes in

■ ask if you can pay by credit card

■ say that you want to cash a traveller's cheque or change some money

When going shopping, work out in advance exactly what you want to ask for. This is the point to check words in your dictionary, rather than later on in the shop, when you feel under pressure. You will find it helpful to calculate the quantities and, if possible, anticipate prices and totals. Rehearse your part of the conversation in your mind.

7

Wo finde ich Geschenke?

- finding the right department
  - ... in a department store
- getting just what you want
- understanding opening times

In Deutschland, in Österreich und in der Schweiz ...

you will find at least one department store
(**das Kaufhaus** or **das Warenhaus**) in any large
town or city. The in-store directory will guide you
to the appropriate department – **die Abteilung**.
Traditionally, shops used to close at lunchtime
on Saturdays, except for one Saturday in the month
(usually the first), when they were open until late
afternoon. This tradition of **langer Samstag** (long
Saturday) is being replaced by more flexible opening
hours and days.

Finding the right department . . .

1 Listen to these key phrases.

wo finde ich . . .   where can I find . . .
. . . Schreibwaren?   . . . stationery?
. . . Geschenke?   . . . gifts?
die Geschenkabteilung ist   the gift department is
. . . im dritten Stock   . . . on the 3rd floor

Auf Deutsch . . .

words are sometimes very long, because they convey ideas which in English would be conveyed by separate words. These compound words become easier to understand and to say if you break them down into their separate parts:

Geschenkabteilung = Geschenk (gift) + **Abteilung**(department)
Mineralwasser   = Mineral (mineral) + **Wasser** (water)

2 **Die Abteilung** (department) can be added to various words:

Sport (sport)   **die Sportabteilung**
Lebensmittel (food)   **die Lebensmittelabteilung**
Süßwaren (confectionery)   **die Süßwarenabteilung**

Can you now write down which department these are sold in?

a **Schreibwaren**   ....
b **Haushaltswaren** (household goods)   ....
c **Lederwaren** (leather goods)   ....

3 Three customers in the new DKP store in Berlin ask where to find various departments. Listen and match the department to the floor.

sports department   first floor
leather goods department   second floor
confectionery department   third floor

. . . in a department store

4 Listen to these key phrases.

wo sind die Toiletten?	where are the toilets?
die Toiletten sind	the toilets are
. . . im Erdgeschoss	. . . on the ground floor
der Parkplatz ist	the car park is
. . . im Untergeschoss	. . . in the basement

Auf Deutsch . . .

'in the' is **in dem** with **der** and **das** words and **in der** with **die** words.

In dem is usually shortened to **im**, as in **im Erdgeschoss**.
In der is not shortened: **in der Geschenkabteilung**.

5 Karen, an assistant in the DKP store, is explaining where some of the store's services are. Listen and decide whether the statements below are true (**richtig**) or false (**falsch**). You should recognise the German for 'restaurant' without difficulty.

a The car park is on the ground floor. ....
b The toilets are on the first floor. ....
c The restaurant is in the basement. ....

6 Listen as Karen gives each customer – **Kunde** (m.) or **Kundin** (f.) – directions. Fill the gaps in their conversations.

a Kunde **Entschuldigen Sie. Wo** .... **die Toiletten?**
     Karen **Die Toiletten? Sie sind** .... ,
            neben dem Parkplatz.

b Kunde **Wo** .... **das Restaurant?**
     Karen **Gegenüber der Bank** ....

c Kundin **Wo finde ich Geschenke?**
     Karen **Die Geschenkabteilung ist** ....

Getting just what you want

1 Listen to these key phrases.

ich suche ein T-Shirt	I'm looking for a T-shirt
das ist zu groß/zu klein	that's too big/too small
die sind zu teuer	those are too expensive
das ist schön	that's nice
ich nehme ein T-Shirt	I'll take a T-shirt

eine Flasche Wein　　**Pralinen**　　　**eine Tasche**

2 Listen to three conversations in a department store and note down in English what each customer wants to buy. Then listen again and note what is said about it (e.g. 'nice'/'too small'). You'll also hear the useful little word **aber**, meaning 'but'.

	Article	Comments
a	....	....
b	....	....
c	....	....

3 Kerstin is doing some shopping, but there is a problem with some of the things she is offered. Listen and tick what you think she will buy.

T-shirt ☐　　wine ☐　　bag ☐　　chocolates ☐

4 How would you say:

- That's too big?
- I'll take a bottle of wine?
- I'm looking for a bag?

Understanding opening times

1 Listen to these key phrases.

wann sind Sie geöffnet?   when are you open?
wir sind . . .   we are . . .
. . . von 9 bis 6 geöffnet   . . . open from 9 a.m. to 6 p.m.
. . . samstags geschlossen   . . . closed on Saturdays
Montag ist Ruhetag   Monday is our rest day

Montag Monday	**Donnerstag** Thurdsay
Dienstag Tuesday	**Freitag** Friday
Mittwoch Wednesday	**Samstag** Saturday
	Sonntag Sunday

Auf Deutsch . . .

adding **s** to any day of the week turns it into 'on -days':

Montag   Monday   **montags**   on Mondays
Samstag   Saturday   **samstags**   on Saturdays

Sonnabend is an alternative word for Saturday used in some areas.

2 Which store is open every day from Monday to Friday?

Ruhetag
mittwochs
a

SAMSTAGS
GESCHLOSSEN
b

Dienstag
Ruhetag
c

3 Kerstin is planning her shopping trip and checks the opening times of the local stores. Listen and note down in English the hours when the stores are open and which day each is closed.

a ....
b ....
c ....

Quiz

1 Which day follows **Dienstag**?
2 Which is the odd one out: **groß**, **teuer**, **geöffnet**, **schön**?
3 Where can you eat: **im Parkplatz**, **im Restaurant** or **in der Lebensmittelabteilung**?
4 What is the assistant telling you? **Wir sind mittwochs geschlossen.**
5 What are the two words for 'Saturday'?
6 Which means 'basement': **Erdgeschoss** or **Untergeschoss**?
7 **Das T-Shirt ist zu groß, die Tasche ist zu klein.** Which item is too big?
8 In which department would you find writing paper?

Now check whether you can . . .

- find your way to various departments in a store

  . . . and the different floors in a building

- describe what you want

- say why something is or isn't suitable

- say you will take something

- ask when a store is open

  . . . and understand opening and closing times

- recognise the days of the week

Remember that a lot of spoken communication is accompanied by gesture and body language. If you don't know the word for the item you want, for example, point to it on the shelf or rail. If you have forgotten how to say that the fit or size is wrong, indicate it with your arms. To be a successful communicator you have to be a bit of a performer. Go ahead and try – you've nothing to lose!

Kontrollpunkt 2

I Match the German and the English.

a	**die Apotheke**	the tourist information office
b	**der Bahnhof**	left
c	**erste Straße rechts**	on the third floor
d	**das Verkehrsamt**	straight ahead
e	**geradeaus**	the station
f	**im dritten Stock**	in the stationery department
g	**das Restaurant**	the chemist's
h	**gegenüber**	the restaurant
i	**links**	opposite
j	**in der Schreibwaren-abteilung**	first road on the right

2 Complete the crossword by putting these words from your shopping list into German.

1 coke
2 coffee
3 biscuits
4 pineapple
5 oranges
6 apple juice
7 bottle
8 bananas
9 can
10 wine
11 tomatoes
12 grapes

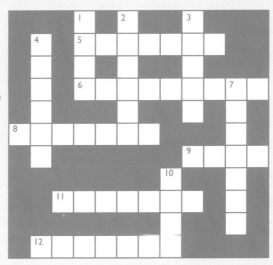

3 Helga has made a shopping list too, but has forgotten to note down the quantities. Choose the most suitable word or phrase on the left to go with each item.

ein Päckchen
sechs Dosen
eine Flasche
eine
ein halbes Kilo
fünf

.... Ananas
.... Cola
.... Trauben
.... Kaffee
.... Orangen
.... Weißwein

4 Listen to some phrases overheard in a department store and check whether the prices you hear are the same as the ones on the tags. Tick the correct ones and change the ones that are wrong.

a € 7,00   d € 14,20   f € 4,50

b € 76,50   e € 14,00   g € 46,00

c € 3,20

5 Frau Braun and Herr Martin are shopping at the local store. Listen and write down what each one buys and the amount they pay.

Frau Braun ....
....

Herr Martin ....
....

6 Three tourists in Munich all ask the way from the market place to the cathedral. Listen to the replies they receive and look at the map on the next page. Which of the three would get to the cathedral, and where would the other two end up?

a ....
b ....
c ....

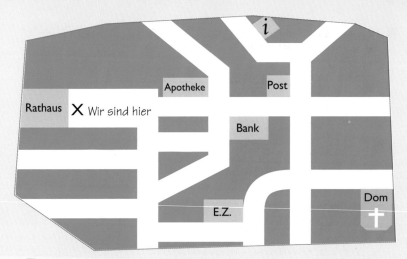

7 Here is part of the store guide (**Wegweiser**) to a large department store.

WEGWEISER	
3. Stock	**Bank**
	Restaurant
2. Stock	**Lederwaren**
1. Stock	**Geschenkabteilung**
Erdgeschoss	**Schreibwaren**
Untergeschoss	**Süßwaren**
	Lebensmittel

Which floor do you need:

a to buy your brother a birthday present? ....

b to buy a handbag? ....

c to change some money? ....

d to buy some envelopes? ....

e to buy some sweets for the children? ....

8 Below is a plan of the third floor of the store. Complete the directions.

a **Die Bank ist gegenüber** ....**.**
b **Die Bank ist neben** .... **.**
c **Die Toiletten** .... **der Sportabteilung.**

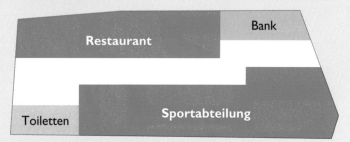

9 Martin has written to a friend, describing his working day. Read the extract from his letter and tick the true statements below.

| Büro office |
| ich arbeite I work |
| Mittagspause midday break |

> Ich habe einen Parkplatz im Untergeschoss und mein Büro
> ist im dritten Stock. Die Sekretärin, Frau Schwarz, hat
> ein Büro im zweiten Stock. Ich arbeite von neun bis eins und
> von zwei bis sechs. Ich habe von eins bis zwei Mittagspause.
> Gegenüber dem Büro ist ein Warenhaus. Das Restaurant
> da ist gut; es ist dienstags bis freitags geöffnet. Montags
> ist Ruhetag und ich gehe zum Café um die Ecke. Es ist
> nicht weit.

a Martin parks his car in the basement.
b Martin's office is on the 3rd floor.
c Frau Schwarz also works in the same office.
d Martin gets an hour and a half for his midday break.
e He usually eats in the restaurant in the department store opposite.
f On Mondays he eats in the café round the corner, but it is a bit far to go.

8 ACHT

Ich möchte ein Zimmer

- checking in at reception
- asking for a hotel room
- booking ahead
- enquiring about facilities

In Deutschland, in Österreich und in der Schweiz . . .

a wide range of accommodation is available: standards are high and prices can be moderate. The best place for help and advice is the tourist office (**Verkehrsamt**), or you can look at the lists of accommodation (**Zimmernachweis**) displayed in public places.

The sign ZIMMER FREI means that rooms are available. There is no all-purpose phrase for 'no vacancies', but the most common expression is **alles besetzt**.

Many English-speaking people assume that a **Gasthaus** is a guest house, whereas it is in fact a pub!

Checking in at reception

1   Listen to these key phrases.

ich habe eine Reservierung für . . .	I've booked . . .
. . . ein Einzelzimmer	. . . a single room
. . . ein Doppelzimmer	. . . a double room
. . . mit Dusche	. . . with a shower
. . . mit Bad	. . . with a bath
hier ist der Schlüssel	here's the key

2   Listen as the receptionist at the Hotel Sonne greets the guests and checks their names in the register. Tick the relevant boxes in the grid and note the room number in the last column.

	Doppelzimmer	Einzelzimmer	Bad	Dusche	Nummer
Friedmann					....
Wolf					....
Lange					....

Auf Deutsch . . .

nicht wahr? and **ja?** are used to check that what you have just said is correct, just as English speakers use 'isn't it?', 'don't you?' and so on. The word **oder?** can be used in the same way.

3   Listen to three more people checking in. This time, note the type of room each has reserved and the floor they are on.

a   Dürnbeck   ....
b   Auerbach   ....
c   Meyer   ....

Which person did you hear being asked their name?

Asking for a hotel room

1 Listen to these key phrases.

haben Sie ein Zimmer frei? have you a room (vacant)?
für wie lange? for how long?
für heute for tonight
für zwei Nächte for two nights
wie schreibt man das? how do you spell that?

2 Listen to three people enquiring about hotel rooms. How long does each one want to stay?

a .... b .... c ....

3 Look at the Pronunciation guide on page 6. Then listen to Kurt saying the German alphabet.
Now listen as he spells his own name. His **Vorname** (first name) is **Kurt**. What is his **Familienname** (surname)?

Familienname: ....

Vorname: Kurt

4 Listen to the rest of the receptionist's conversation with the three guests in activity 2. Write their names as they spell them.

a .... b .... c ....

Now practise spelling your own name.

5 How would you say:

● have you a room for tonight?
● a single room for four nights, please.
● have you a double room for three nights?

Booking ahead

1   Listen to these key phrases.

ich möchte ein Zimmer reservieren   I'd like to book a room
für wann?   when for?
vom zweiten . . .   from the second . . .
. . . bis zum vierten   . . . until the fourth
es tut mir leid   I'm sorry
das Hotel ist voll besetzt   the hotel is full

Januar January	**Februar** February	**März** March	**April** April
Mai May	**Juni** June	**Juli** July	**August** August
September September	**Oktober** October	**November** November	**Dezember** December

Auf Deutsch . . .

you use 'first', 'second', 'third', etc. both to give dates and to say what floor something is on.
From 1st to 19th you add **-ten** to the number:
    zwei + ten = zweiten (2nd); **vier + ten = vierten** (4th)
There are four exceptions:
    ersten (1st), **dritten** (3rd), **siebten** (7th), **achten** (8th)
From 20th onwards, you add **-sten** instead:
    vierundzwanzig + sten = vierundzwanzigsten (24th)
The abbreviated form uses a full stop: **1.** = 1st, **2.** = 2nd, and so on.

2   Listen to the receptionist at the Hotel Sonne taking bookings over the phone. What dates are the rooms wanted for?

a ....   *b* ....   *c* ....

Which customer will be disappointed?

Enquiring about facilities

1   Listen to these key phrases.

gibt es ein Schwimmbad?	is there a swimming pool?
gibt es eine Bank in der Nähe?	is there a bank nearby?
es gibt einen Parkplatz	there is a car park
wann ist Frühstück?	when is breakfast?
bis wann ist die Bar geöffnet?	until when is the bar open?

2   Listen as some guests make enquiries at the reception desk and note in English what each person asks.

a ....

b ....

c ....

d ....

3   Listen again and write the information they receive next to their question above. **Hinter dem Hotel** means 'behind the hotel'.

Auf Deutsch . . .

es gibt means both 'there is' and 'there are'
gibt es? means both 'is there?' and 'are there?'

4   Brigitte is telling her tour party about the Hotel Sonne. Listen and note the information in English. **Abends** is of course 'in the evening'.

a   breakfast times   ....

b   restaurant hours   ....

c   location of bar   ....

d   location of swimming pool   ....

Listen again: how long will the party be staying?

Put it all together

I Read the memo about Hans Kraus, who is visiting a German company. Fill in the hotel form for him; you should be able to guess what the unfamiliar words mean.

Memorandum

Hans Kraus ist Architekt. Er ist im Hotel Bach in Leipzig vom elften bis zum achtzehnten September. Er hat Zimmer Nummer sechsundsiebzig. Herr Kraus ist Holländer.

HOTEL BACH

Familienname: .... Vorname: ....

Beruf: .... Nationalität: ....

Zimmernummer: .... vom: .... bis zum: ....

2 Complete the sentences with the help of the symbols.

a **Ich habe eine Reservierung für** ....

b **Gibt es** ....?

c **Wann ist** ....?

d **Ich habe eine Reservierung vom** ....

P

1/3 – 4/3

3 Match the German to the English.

a	**Für wann?**	For how long?
b	**Haben Sie ein Zimmer frei?**	nearby
c	**Das Hotel ist voll besetzt.**	behind the hotel
d	**in der Nähe**	When for?
e	**hinter dem Hotel**	The hotel's full.
f	**Für wie lange?**	Have you a room?

Now you're talking!

I   Take the part of Hannelore Förster, arriving at the Hotel Ludwig.

  ◇ **Guten Tag. Kann ich Ihnen helfen?**
  ◆ Greet the receptionist and ask if they have a room.
  ◇ **Ein Einzelzimmer oder ein Doppelzimmer?**
  ◆ Say a single room with a bathroom.
  ◇ **Für wie lange?**
  ◆ Say for three nights.
  ◇ **Gut. Also Zimmer dreiundneunzig im zweiten Stock.**

2   Now take the part of this hotel guest.

  ◆ Greet the receptionist and say you've booked a room.
  ◇ **Wie heißen Sie?**
  ◆ Give your name.
  ◇ **Ein Doppelzimmer mit Dusche, nicht wahr?**
  ◆ Say yes, and when you want it for.
  ◇ **Gut. Hier ist der Schlüssel, Herr Wilson.**
  ◆ Ask if there's a car park nearby.
  ◇ **Ja, hinter dem Hotel.**

James Wilson

Hotel zum
Goldenen Löwen

Double room
with shower

19/6–26/6

3   This time you ring the Eurotel to book a room.

  ◇ **Guten Morgen. Eurotel Dresden.**
  ◆ Say good morning, you'd like to book a room.
  ◇ **Für wann?**
  ◆ Say for tonight.
  ◇ **Für wie lange?**
  ◆ Say until the twelfth.
  ◇ **Ja, wie heißen Sie, bitte?**
  ◆ Say your name.
  ◇ **Wie schreibt man das?**
  ◆ Give the information.

Quiz

1 Which month follows **Februar?**
2 Write down the dates you are staying: **vom dritten bis zum neunten Mai**.
3 What information do you want if you ask **Wann ist Frühstück?**
4 How would you ask: 'Is there a swimming pool nearby?'
5 Which is your surname: **Vorname** or **Familienname?**
6 If someone says **für fünf Nächte**, how long are they staying?
7 What do you do if someone asks **Wie schreibt man das?**
8 If someone says **Es tut mir leid**, are they expressing pleasure, regret or anger?

Now check whether you can . . .

■ say that you've booked a room

■ ask if a room is available

■ book a room by phone

■ specify the kind of room you want

■ say how long you want the room for and give precise dates

■ spell your name in German

■ understand the spelling of other people's names

■ ask about hotel facilities

Before you listen to or take part in a recorded conversation, imagine yourself in that situation. What would you say if you were in a hotel in England, for example? This helps you to anticipate what people will say in German and makes it easier to understand what you hear.

9

Wann fährt der nächste Zug?

- asking about public transport
  - . . . and arrival and departure times
- buying tickets and checking travel details

In Deutschland, in Österreich und in der Schweiz . . .

public transport is generally clean, quick and reliable. In many cities there is a wide variety of means of transport: you can travel **mit der Straßenbahn** (by tram), **mit dem Bus** (by bus) or **mit der U-Bahn** (by underground). Most towns and cities have an integrated transport system, where one ticket is valid for all forms of public transport within the city limits. In many places you can also travel on local waterways, **mit der Fähre** (by ferry) or **mit dem Dampfer** (by steamer).

Asking about public transport . . .

1 Listen to these key phrases.

wo ist die Bushaltestelle?	where is the bus stop?
fährt diese Straßenbahn . . .	does this tram go . . .
welche Linie fährt . . .	which number/line goes . . .
. . . zum Stadion?	. . . to the stadium?
. . . zur Stadtmitte?	. . . to the town centre?
. . . nach Garmisch?	. . . to Garmisch?

2 Listen to various people in **München** (Munich) asking how to get to places by tram, and complete the grid below.

	a	b	c	d
Number	5	....	....	....
Place	....	....	Schwabing	station

Auf Deutsch . . .

nach is always used for 'to' with place names:
> **nach Hamburg, nach Boston**

zu is used with other places and its ending varies according to the gender (**der, die, das**) of the word:
> **zum Bahnhof (der), zur Apotheke (die), zum Rathaus (das)**

3 Listen to the conversation in a Munich street and fill the gaps below. Where does the visitor (**Besucher**) want to go, and how will he get there?

Besucher	**Fährt diese** .... **zum Rathaus, bitte?**
Frau	**Nein,** .... **Schwabing. Der Bus** .... **zum Rathaus. Dort drüben ist die** ....
Besucher	**Welche** .... **fährt** .... **Rathaus?**
Frau	**Die** .... **fünf.**

. . . and arrival and departure times

4 Listen to these key phrases.

wann fährt der nächste Zug?	when does the next train go?
der Zug nach Berlin . . .	the train to Berlin . . .
. . . fährt um sieben Uhr	. . . goes at seven o'clock
wann kommt der Zug in Bonn an?	when does the train arrive in Bonn?
um dreizehn Uhr dreißig	at 13:30

5 Listen to the announcements at Linz's main station and write the times of the arrivals and departures in the correct box.

	Abfahrt (Departure)	**Ankunft** (Arrival)
Siegen		
Linz		
Zürich		
Leipzig		

Auf Deutsch . . .

certain verbs, like **ankommen** (to arrive), can split into two parts: **an** and **kommen**. **An** goes at the end of the sentence: **Wann kommt der Zug/Bus in ... an?** Don't forget to include it!

6 In the Munich tourist office, people are asking about transport. Listen and complete the grid in English.

Place	Time	Transport
Garmisch	....	....
Schwabing	....	....
Stadium	....	....
Town centre	....	....

Buying tickets . . .

1   Listen to these key phrases.

einmal nach München	one (ticket) to Munich
einfach . . .	single . . .
. . . oder hin und zurück?	. . . or return?
zweimal erster Klasse	two first class (tickets)
dreimal zweiter Klasse	three second class (tickets)

Auf Deutsch . . .

the word for ticket (**Fahrkarte**) is not normally used when actually buying one. Instead, **-mal** is added to the number of tickets needed: **einmal zweiter Klasse einfach nach Berlin**. The pattern 'number, class, type, destination' is a useful one to learn.

2   There's a queue of people buying train tickets at **Köln** (Cologne) station. Listen: how many do they want? First or second class? Write the numbers in the grid. Then listen again: what type of ticket do they ask for?

Destination	Number	Class	Type
Innsbruck	....	....	....
Potsdam	....	....	....
Augsburg	....	....	....
Vaduz	....	....	....
Basel	....	....	....

3   How would you ask for these tickets? (Remember the pattern.)

● single tickets for two people first class to Munich
● a return ticket to Innsbruck for one person, second class
● four second class singles to Mainz
● three returns to Mannheim, second class

. . . and checking travel details

4 Listen to these key phrases.

muss ich umsteigen?	do I have to change?
wo muss ich aussteigen?	where must I get off?
kann ich einen Platz reservieren?	can I reserve a seat?
von welchem Gleis fährt der Zug?	which platform does the train go from?

5 Listen to the travellers making enquiries at the Cologne booking office and note down where each person wants to go. Listen again and note what additional information they ask for. (The employee's **Ja, sicher** means 'Yes, of course'.)

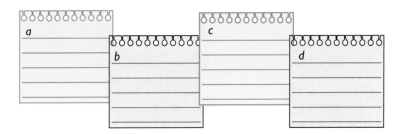

6 Find the appropriate response to each question.

a	**Muss ich umsteigen?**	**Von Gleis 7.**
b	**Kann ich einen Platz reservieren?**	**In Berlin.**
c	**Von welchem Gleis fährt der Zug?**	**Ja, sicher.**
d	**Wo muss ich aussteigen?**	**Ja, in Köln.**

7 What questions would you ask to find out:

● if you need to change?
● what platform the train leaves from?
● where to get off?

Put it all together

1 Two conversations have got mixed up. Recreate them by numbering the sentences A 1 to 4 and B 1 to 4.

Conversation A: **Buying a ticket**

Conversation B: **At the bus stop**

....		**Und wo ist die Bushaltestelle für die Linie 7?**
....		**Nach Bonn? Ja, einfach oder hin und zurück?**
....		**Die Linie 7 zur Stadtmitte? Um 17:00.**
....		**Da drüben, gegenüber dem Rathaus.**
....		**€ 28,40 einmal einfach nach Bonn.**
....	B1	**Wann fährt der Bus zur Stadtmitte, bitte?**
....	A1	**Einmal nach Bonn, bitte.**
....		**Einfach, bitte.**

2 Practise saying the following times and then write them out in words.

a 14:40   *b* 16:30   *c* 12:05   *d* 07:15

3 Fill in the appropriate question words.

a **Von** .... **Gleis fährt der Zug?**   **Von Gleis 3.**
b .... **fährt der Zug nach Berlin?**   **Um 12:30.**
c .... **ist die Straßenbahnhaltestelle?**   **Dort drüben.**
d .... **Linie fährt zum Stadion?**   **Die Linie 8.**
e .... **muss ich umsteigen?**   **In Berlin.**

4 Complete these sentences with the correct word for 'to'.

a **Mein Mann fährt heute** .... **Innsbruck.**
b **Die Straßenbahn fährt** .... **Stadtmitte.**
c **Welche Linie fährt** .... **Stadion?**
d **Der Zug fährt** .... **München.**

"Now you're talking!

1   You're staying in Munich and want to make an outing to Bad Tölz by train. You go to the main station (**der Hauptbahnhof**) and hear this announcement.

◇ **Der nächste Zug nach Bad Tölz fährt in** .... **von** .... **ab.**

You didn't catch the details, so you go to the ticket office.

◆ Ask when the train leaves.

◇ **In zwanzig Minuten, um 13:25.**

◆ Ask which platform it leaves from.

◇ **Von Gleis vier.**

◆ Ask for a second class return ticket.

2   While you wait, you go to the advance booking office to get the ticket for your trip to Hamburg.

◆ Say you want a single second class ticket to Hamburg.

◇ **Nach Hamburg?**

◆ Say yes and ask how much it costs.

◇ **Es kostet € 90.**

◆ Ask if you can reserve a seat.

◇ **Ja, sicher.**

3   You also want to visit the Stadttheater in Oberammergau. Prepare what you need to ask, using the notes below, then take part in the conversation on the cassette. You want to know:

◆ where the bus stop is

◆ what a return ticket costs

◆ the time of the next bus

◆ the time of arrival in Oberammergau

◆ where you have to get off

◆ if it's far to the Stadttheater

◆ when the bus back to Munich leaves.

Quiz

1 You are told **Sie müssen in Koblenz umsteigen.** What must you do?

2 You hear **von Gleis zwölf** – are you at the railway station or the bus stop?

3 What is the German for 'bus route/number'?

4 How do you say 'to the station'?

5 What do you know about this train? **der Zug nach Bonn**

6 Which board tells you about arrivals: the one headed **Ankunft** or **Abfahrt**?

7 How do you say 'by tram': **mit der U-Bahn, mit der Fähre** or **mit der Straßenbahn**?

8 How do you ask about reserving a seat? **Kann ich .... reservieren?**

Now check whether you can . . .

■ ask about transport to places in town

■ ask about transport to other towns and cities

■ ask about arrival and departure times

■ ask for single and return tickets

■ ask if you can book a seat

■ ask whether you have to change

■ ask where to get off

■ understand straightforward replies to all these questions

There are often several ways of saying the same thing, so it's a good idea in the early stages to learn the patterns given in the units even if you then hear other expressions being used. As you progress and gain confidence you can, of course, begin to experiment with other patterns.

10 ZEHN

Guten Appetit!

- reading the menu
- ordering a meal
- choosing cakes and desserts
- finishing the meal

In Deutschland, in Österreich und in der Schweiz . . .

the quality and variety of food is generally good. In every region you will find many local specialities (**Spezialitäten**) and different types of bread, beer, sausage (**Wurst**), ham (**Schinken**) and cheese (**Käse**). Cakes and gateaux are popular everywhere as desserts, and are also enjoyed with coffee at other times of the day. A visit to the **Konditorei** (cake shop, usually with café) is to be recommended.

In German households the main meal of the day still tends to be at midday, and the evening meal often consists of soup (**Suppe**) or cold meats (**Aufschnitt**). Both at home and when eating out, it is customary to begin the meal by saying **Guten Appetit!** (Enjoy your meal!)

Reading the menu

I   Listen to these key phrases.

die Speisekarte, bitte	the menu, please
was ist . . . ?	what is . . . ?
was für Fleisch ist das?	what kind of meat is it?
ist das Rindfleisch?	is it beef?
ist das Schweinefleisch . . .	is it pork . . .
. . . oder Kalbfleisch?	. . . or veal?

2   Three people at the Restaurant Alpenblick are asking about unfamiliar dishes. Listen and note the type of meat they contain.

Sauerbraten   ....
Weißwurst   ....
Jägerschnitzel   ....

3   The secret of understanding a menu is to home in on the words you think you recognise and make inspired guesses! Look at these starters (**Vorspeisen**) and main courses (**Hauptgerichte**) and decide what each dish contains. If in doubt, check with the glossary.

SPEISEKARTE *Restaurant Alpenblick*

VORSPEISEN
a   **Heringssalat**
b   **Krabbencocktail**
c   **Melone mit Schinken**

HAUPTGERICHTE
d   **Rumpsteak**
e   **Kalbsleber**
f   **Schweinekotelett**
g   **Rinderbraten**
h   **Großer Salat mit Tunfisch**

Ordering a meal

1 Listen to these key phrases.

was ist die Tagessuppe?   what is the soup of the day?
was empfehlen Sie?   what do you recommend?
das Hähnchen ist gut   the chicken is good
und zum Trinken . . . ?   and to drink . . . ?

2 Listen as Helga and Kurt order a meal from the waitress (**Kellnerin**) and fill the gaps below. Listen out for **also**, one of those filler words, meaning 'in that case'. What do you think **Salat** is?

Kellnerin   **Bitte schön?**
Helga   **Was** .... **Sie?**
Kellnerin   **Der Sauerbraten und das Hähnchen mit Salat sind**

            .... **.**
Helga   **Ich nehme das Hähnchen.**
Kurt   **Und was ist die** .... **?**
Kellnerin   **Tomatensuppe.**
Kurt   **Also eine Tomatensuppe und zwei Hähnchen.**

3 Helga and Kurt are still talking to the waitress. Listen and note down in English what each orders.

Helga   ....

Kurt   ....

4 Three other customers at the Alpenblick restaurant are deciding what to order. Listen to their conversations and answer the questions.

- Which customer, a, b or c, asks for a recommendation?
- How many of them have starters?
- What is the pork chop served with?
- Who has fish followed by chicken?
- Do they order chicken with rice (**Reis**) or chips (**Pommes frites**)?

Choosing cakes and desserts

I   Listen to these key phrases.

als Nachspeise nehme ich . . .	for dessert I'll have . . .
. . . gemischtes Eis	. . . mixed ice cream
. . . ein Stück Nusstorte	. . . a piece of nut gateau
wir haben frisches Obst	we have fresh fruit

2   Two customers are looking at the Alpenblick's dessert menu. Listen to their conversation and tick the items they choose. Before listening, look up the two new words in the glossary.

> NACHSPEISEN
> Käsekuchen
> Nusstorte
> Schokoladentorte
> gemischtes Eis mit Sahne
> frisches Obst

3   Listen to a customer in the Konditorei Ralf ordering for herself and two friends. Which of the three orders below is hers?

a
> 1 nut gateau
> 1 chocolate ice
>   cream with cream
> 1 chocolate cake
> 3 coffees

b
> 1 nut gateau with
>   cream
> 1 chocolate cake
>   with cream
> 1 fruit gateau
> 3 coffees

c
> 1 fruit gateau
> 1 nut gateau with
>   cream
> 1 chocolate cake
> 3 coffees

Finishing the meal

I Listen to these key phrases.

hat's geschmeckt?	did you enjoy your meal?
ja, es hat gut geschmeckt	yes, it was good
die Rechnung, bitte	the bill, please
das macht € 54,70	that comes to € 54,70
zahlen Sie bitte an der Kasse	please pay at the cash desk
das ist für Sie	here's something for you

2 Helga and Kurt have finished their meal and call the waitress over to their table. Listen to the conversation.

- *a* What did they have for dessert?
- *b* Where do they pay?
- *c* Do they leave a tip?
- *d* Which of the following is their bill?

€ 73,20	€ 27,30	€ 23,70	€ 72,30

3 Listen to the customer at the next table and fill the blanks in his conversation with the waitress below. What is he asking when he says **Was macht das?**

Mann	**Die ...., bitte.**
Fräulein	**Ja, gut. Hat's ....?**
Mann	**Ja, es hat .... Was macht das?**
Fräulein	**Das .... € 36.**
Mann	**Danke. Das ist ....**

4 What would you say:

- when you want the bill?
- when you give a tip?
- when you have enjoyed your meal?

Put it all together

1   Put the following items in the right place on the menu.

Vorspeisen	Hauptgerichte	Nachspeisen
....	....	....
....	....	....
....	....	....
....	....	....

Schweinekotelett	**Heringssalat**	**Tomatensuppe**
Käsekuchen	**Hähnchen**	**Kalbsleber**
gemischtes Eis	**Rinderbraten**	**Tunfischsalat**
Apfelkuchen	**frisches Obst**	

2   Number the sentences in the correct order to make a conversation between a customer and a waitress.

a   **Das ist Kalbfleisch.**   ....
b   **Ein Glas Apfelsaft.**   ....
c   **Bitte schön.**   ....
d   **Gut, also Schnitzel mit Pommes frites, bitte.** ....
e   **Die Speisekarte, bitte.**   ....
f   **Und zum Trinken?**   ....
g   **Wiener Schnitzel – was für Fleisch ist das?** ....

3   Find the appropriate response to each of a to f.

a   **Und zum Trinken?**   **Das ist Kalbfleisch.**
b   **Und als Nachspeise?**   **Einen Viertelliter Weißwein, bitte.**
c   **Hat's geschmeckt?**   **Der Fisch ist gut.**
d   **Was macht das?**   **Ich nehme gemischtes Eis.**
e   **Was empfehlen Sie?**   **Es hat gut geschmeckt.**
f   **Was ist Weißwurst?**   **€ 45,20.**

"Now you're talking!

1   You arrive in a restaurant and take a seat.

- ◆ Ask for the menu.
- ◇ **Bitte schön.**
- ◆ Point to an unfamiliar item (**Eisbein**). Ask what type of meat it is.
- ◇ **Eisbein – das ist Schweinefleisch.**
- ◆ You don't like pork; order chicken with rice.
- ◇ **Und zum Trinken?**
- ◆ Ask for a glass of mineral water.

2   On another occasion you find it difficult to choose.

- ◆ Ask what they recommend.
- ◇ **Der Fisch ist heute sehr frisch.**
- ◆ Say good, in that case the fish please.
- ◇ **Mit Salat oder Pommes frites?**
- ◆ Say you would like salad.

3   When the waitress brings the meal, she wishes you
- ◇ **Guten Appetit!**

Later she returns and asks:
- ◇ **Hat's geschmeckt?**
- ◆ Say yes, and as dessert you'll have fresh fruit.
- ◇ **Und sonst noch etwas?**
- ◆ Say you'd like a pot of coffee with cream.

4   Now you've finished your meal.
- ◆ Say you want the bill.
- ◇ **Also . . . Fisch mit Salat, frisches Obst und ein Kännchen Kaffee . . . Das macht € 13,60.**

As you are about to offer her the money, she says
- ◇ **Zahlen Sie bitte an der Kasse.**
- ◆ Offer her a tip.
- ◇ **Danke schön. Auf Wiedersehen.**

Quiz

1 Which is the odd one out: **Rinderbraten**, **Rumpsteak** or **Schweinekotelett**?
2 What do you say to people as they start their meal?
3 In what order do these appear on a menu? **Hauptgerichte**, **Nachspeisen**, **Vorspeisen**
4 Which is made of veal: **Jägerschnitzel** or **Wiener Schnitzel**?
5 How do you tell someone the meal was good?
6 Which of these would you choose if you were a vegetarian: **Hähnchen**, **Tomatensuppe** or **Schinken**?
7 You go to the **Kasse** – what do you do there?
8 When do you say **Das ist für Sie**?

Now check whether you can . . .

■ work out what the main items on a menu are

■ ask about items on the menu

■ order a meal with drinks

■ say that you enjoyed your meal

■ ask for the bill

■ offer the waiter/waitress a tip

Before going out to eat in a German restaurant, it's a good idea to look up in the dictionary any food or drink you don't like, such as liver (**Leber**), kidneys (**Nieren**), onions (**Zwiebeln**), or garlic (**Knoblauch**). That way you can avoid disappointments!

And now, congratulations on reaching the end of *Talk German*. Prepare yourself for the final **Kontrollpunkt** with some revision. Listen to the conversations again – the more you listen the more confident you will become – and use the quizzes and checklists to assess how much you can remember. And take every opportunity to speak German; if no one else is available, talk aloud to yourself!

Kontrollpunkt 3

You've arrived in a small South German town at the start of your holiday.

I You take a taxi to your hotel, the Hotel Adler, and talk to Maria, the receptionist. Fill the gaps in your conversation with the appropriate word or phrase from the box.

You	**Guten Abend. Ich habe eine** .... **.**
Maria	**Wie** ...., **bitte?**
You	**Mein** .... **ist** .... **.**
Maria	**Ach ja, ein Einzelzimmer mit Bad, nicht wahr?**
You	**Nein, nein, ein Einzelzimmer** .... **.**
Maria	**Oh, entschuldigen Sie, und bis wann?**
You	**Bis** .... **.**

> **mit Dusche**
> **Reservierung**
> **zum neunten**
> **Name**
> **heißen Sie**
> **[your name]**

2 Once in your room, you decide to ring reception for some information. Work out how you will ask the following, then listen to check your questions and note down the information given.

a When is breakfast? ....
b Where is the bar? ....
c When is the bar open? ....
d Is there a swimming pool in the hotel? ....

3 Next day you want to go on a day trip by ferry across the lake to Konstanz. You ask for details at reception. For each question choose the correct options.

a **Wann fährt die U-Bahn/die Straßenbahn/ die Fähre nach Konstanz?**
b **Wann geht/kommt/fährt sie in Konstanz an?**
c **Was kostet es einfach/hin und zurück?**

8 In your hotel room you find some brochures and advertisements. Read them and see if you can answer the questions. There are some unfamiliar words – look them up in the glossary if you need to.

   a Which restaurants are closed one day in the week and which days are they closed in each case?

   b Where can you park for the **Rathauskeller**?

   c Where exactly is the **Rathauskeller**?

   d Where can you eat local specialities?

   e Which restaurant stays open latest and on which days?

   f Which two restaurants also offer accommodation?

   g Next to the items on your shopping list below, write the name of the department you will need and the floor it is on in the **Kaufcenter**.

leather gloves	....	....
local sausage	....	....
notepaper	....	....
box of chocolates	....	....
bottle of perfume	....	....

   h What else can you buy in the basement?

   i Where is the earliest pick-up point for the Neuschwanstein excursion?

   j What happens at 1.00 p.m.?

   k How long is the coffee break?

   l Where do you arrive at 8.40 p.m.?

Haus Vogtland
Restaurant und kleines Hotel

Montag 09.00–14.00 und
17.00–22.00

Mittwoch–Samstag 9–22

Sonntag 9–20

Dienstag Ruhetag

10 Zimmer. Nur Apr.–Okt.
geöffnet

ZUM GOLDENEN LÖWEN
....

- 50 Zimmer mit Bad oder Dusche, Telefon, TV
- Geöffnet bis 23 Uhr
- Kinderspielplatz, Minigolf, Terrasse
- Parkplatz hinter dem Haus

RESTAURANT RATHAUSKELLER
Lokale Spezialitäten – Internationale Gerichte

Ruhetag: Montag

Geöffnet: Dienstag–Freitag 12.00–22.00 Uhr

Samstag u. Sonntag 12.00–24.00 Uhr

In der Altstadt gegenüber dem Dom
Parken auf dem Marktplatz

KAUFCENTER

2. Stock	Lederwaren Männermode Toiletten
1. Stock	Geschenke Parfum Frauenmode
Erdgeschoss	Schreibwaren Süßwaren
Untergeschoss	Lebensmittel Wein

Busfahrt nach Neuschwanstein

Abfahrt:	09.00	Hinter dem Rathaus
	09.10	Neben der Post
	09.20	Hotel Sonne

Kaffeepause: 11.00-11.30 in Königsstadt

Ankunft in Neuschwanstein: 13.00

Tour: 14.30

Abfahrt: 17.30

Ankunft:	20.30	Hotel Sonne
	20.40	Neben der Post
	20.50	Hinter dem Rathaus

Audio scripts and answers

This section contains transcripts of all the conversations. Answers which consist of words and phrases from the conversations are given in bold type in the transcripts. Other answers are given separately, after each activity.

Unit I **Guten Tag!**

Pages 8 & 9 **Saying hello and goodbye**

2 *a* Guten Morgen, Frau Müller.
b Tag, Rudi.
c Guten Abend, Herr Braun.
d Morgen, Frau Schmidt.
e Guten Tag, Herr Scholz.
a morning; b afternoon; c evening; d morning; e afternoon

3 First name: 1; Herr: 2; Frau: 2

5 *a* ● Guten Abend, Herr Braun. Wie geht es Ihnen?
● Gut, danke, und Ihnen?
● Gut, danke.
b ● Abend, Ulla. Wie geht's?
● Gut, danke.
c ● Guten Abend, Rudi. Wie geht's?
● Gut, danke.
The people in b and c know each other well.

7 ● **Auf Wiedersehen!**
● **Tschüs**, Maria.
● **Gute Nacht**, Rudi.
● **Wiedersehen**, Frau Engel.

8 *a* Tschüs, Helga, gute Nacht.
b Guten Abend, Frau Onken. Wie geht es Ihnen?
c Guten Abend, Herr Kunz.
d Wiedersehen, Hannelore.
e Auf Wiedersehen, Herr Brammerts.
The people in a, d and e are leaving.

9 Morgen, Barbara.
Guten Abend, Herr Scholz.
Guten Morgen, Frau Hoffmann.
Tag, Manfred.
Guten Abend, Rudi.
Barbara: Wie geht's?/Herr Scholz: Wie geht es Ihnen?
Manfred: Tschüs./Rudi: (Auf) Wiedersehen.

Pages 10 & 11 **Introducing yourself and socializing**

2 ● Guten **Tag**. Mein Name ist **Müller, Heinrich Müller**.
● Guten Tag, Herr Müller.
● Guten **Abend**, ich heiße **Blum, Anna**.
● Ja, guten Abend, Frau Blum.
● Guten **Abend**, ich heiße **Barbara Goldmann**.
● Guten Abend, Frau Goldmann.
● Guten **Tag**. Mein Name ist **Brammerts**.
● Guten Tag, Herr Brammerts.

3 ● Guten Tag. Wie heißen Sie, bitte?
● **Ich heiße** Altmann, Georg Altmann.

6 ● Wie heißen **Sie**?
● Ich **heiße** Georg Altmann. Und Sie?
● Mein **Name** ist Schwarz, Maria Schwarz.
● Wie bitte?
● Maria Schwarz.
● **Freut mich**, Frau Schwarz.

8 *a* ● Tag, **Jutta**. Wie geht's?
● Gut, danke, **Liesl**.
b ● Guten Tag. Ich heiße **Dieter** Scholz.
● Guten Tag, Herr Scholz.
c ● Wie heißen Sie?
● Ich heiße **Manfred**.
d ● Und mein Name ist **Kerstin**. Wie heißen Sie?
● Mein Name ist **Inge**.

Page 12 **Put it all together**

1 *a* Goodbye; *b* What's your name?;
c 'bye; *d* Good afternoon; *e* Pardon;
f Good night; *g* Pleased to meet you;
h How are you?

2 *a* Guten Morgen; *b* Guten Abend;
c Guten Tag; *d* Tschüs

3 *c, b, e, a, d*

Page 13 **Now you're talking!**

1 • **Guten Tag.**
 • Guten Tag. Wie geht es Ihnen?
 • **Gut, danke. Und Ihnen?**
 • Gut, danke.

2 • **Guten Tag! Ich heiße (your
 name).**
 • Freut mich. Ich heiße Schneider, Anna
 Schneider.
 • **Wie bitte?**
 • Frau Schneider, Anna Schneider.
 • **Es freut mich, Frau Schneider.**

3 • **Guten Tag. Wie heißen Sie,
 bitte?**
 • Mein Name ist Offenbach.
 • **Es freut mich, Herr Offenbach.
 Ich heiße (your name).**

4 • **Auf Wiedersehen, Frau
 Schneider. Auf Wiedersehen,
 Herr Offenbach.**

5 • **Auf Wiedersehen, Frau Meyer,
 gute Nacht.**

Page 14 **Quiz**

1 When saying goodbye to someone
you know well; *2* Ich heiße …;
3 Mein Name ist …; *4* When you
haven't heard/understood something;
5 Es freut mich; *6* Gute Nacht;
7 Wie geht's? *8* Morning

Unit 2 **Woher kommen Sie?**

Pages 16 & 17 **Saying where you're
from and where your home town is**

2 • Woher kommen Sie?
 • **Ich bin Engländer.**
 • Und Sie? Woher kommen Sie?
 • Ich komme aus Irland.
 • Gut. Und Sie? Kommen Sie aus
 England?
 • Nein, ich komme aus Wales. Ich bin
 Waliserin.
 • Sind Sie Engländer?
 • **Ja, ich bin Engländer.**
 Two of the people are English.

3/4 • Ich bin **Spanier.**
 • Ich komme aus Italien. Ich bin
 Italienerin.
 • Ich bin **Schottin.**
 • Ich bin **Kanadierin.**
 • Ich komme aus Australien. Ich bin
 Australier.
 • Ich bin **Irin.**
 • Ich bin **Amerikaner.**
 • Ich bin **Österreicherin.**
 There are 3 men and 5 women.
 Spanish, Italian, Scottish, Canadian,
 Australian, Irish, American, Austrian

6 • Ich heiße Peter Davies. Ich wohne in
 Cardiff in **Wales.**
 • Mein Name ist Irene Fischer. Ich
 wohne in **Hamburg** in
 Deutschland.
 • Ich komme aus **Perth** in
 Schottland. Mein Name ist John
 McPhee.
 • Mein Name ist Maeve Sullivan. Ich
 wohne in **Waterford** in **Irland.**

7 • Wo **wohnen** Sie, Frau Schwarz?
 • Ich **wohne** in Wien in Österreich.
 • **Wo** wohnen Sie?
 • Ich wohne **in** Bozen in **Italien.**
 • Und wo wohnen **Sie?** Sind Sie
 Italiener?
 • Nein, ich bin Spanier. **Ich** wohne in
 Madrid.

Page 18 Saying what you do

2 policewoman = Polizistin; student = Student; computer programmer = Programmierer; 3 refer to women.

3 • Frau Sullivan, was sind Sie?
 • Ich bin **Lehrerin**.
 • Und was sind Sie, Frau Fischer?
 • Ich bin **Hausfrau**.
 • Herr Smith, was sind Sie?
 • Ich bin **Sekretär**.
 • Und was sind Sie, Frau Pastena?
 • Ich bin **Polizistin**.
 • Und Sie, Herr McPhee?
 • Ich bin **Programmierer**.
 • Und was sind Sie, Herr Davies?
 • Ich bin **Student**.
 teacher, housewife, secretary, policewoman, computer programmer, student

Page 19 Using the numbers from 0 to 10

2 **drei**; neun; vier; **sechs**; **acht**; fünf

3 • Was ist Ihre Telefonnummer, Frau Fischer?
 • **Vier, sechs, zwo, fünf, drei, acht**.
 • Was ist Ihre Telefonnummer, Herr Smith?
 • **Acht, zwo, drei, neun, fünf, eins**.
 • Und Ihre Telefonnummer, Herr Davies?
 • **Sechs, sieben, eins, fünf, zwo, sechs**.
 Irene: 462538; Mark: 823951; Peter: 671526

4 • Sieben, null, vier, fünf, sechs, acht.
 • Fünf, neun, eins, sechs, sieben, vier.
 • Eins, zwo, fünf, drei, sechs, sieben, drei, zwo.
 • Acht, fünf, drei, eins, neun, sieben.

Page 20 Put it all together

1 *a* Ich bin Kanadier; *b* Aus Amerika; *c* Nein, ich komme aus Irland; *d* Ich wohne in Stirling;

e Ich bin Hausfrau; *f* 01982 46723
2 Helen Brownsmith: American; Washington; teacher
 Georg Müller: Austrian; Salzburg; computer programmer
 Andrew Hyde: Scottish; Glasgow; policeman

3 Ich heiße Dieter Hoffmann. Ich bin Österreicher und ich wohne in Wien. Ich bin arbeitslos.
 Ich heiße Juanita Pueblos. Ich bin Spanierin. Ich wohne in Madrid und ich bin Studentin.

Page 21 Now you're talking!

1 • Sind Sie Ausländerin?
 • **Ja, ich bin Amerikanerin**.
 • Wo wohnen Sie?
 • **Ich wohne in Washington**.
 • Was sind Sie?
 • **Ich bin Lehrerin**.

2 • Herr Jones, sind Sie Engländer?
 • **Nein, ich bin Waliser**.
 • Wo wohnen Sie in Wales?
 • **Ich wohne in Cardiff**.
 • Was sind Sie?
 • **Ich bin Mechaniker**.
 • Und was ist Ihre Telefonnummer?
 • **Null, eins, sechs, vier, drei, neun, sieben, fünf, acht**.

3 • **Wie heißen Sie?**
 • Ich heiße Ulrike Dietrich.
 • **Wo wohnen Sie?**
 • Ich wohne in Kiel in Deutschland.
 • **Was sind Sie?**
 • Ich bin Stewardess bei Lufthansa.

Page 22 Quiz

1 Ich bin Amerikanerin; *2* Wohnen Sie in Leipzig? *3* Ich komme aus Chester; *4* Nein, ich bin (your nationality); *5* Ich bin Studentin; *6* Austria; *7* vier, sieben; *8* Schottin

Unit 3 **Zwei Kaffee, bitte**

Pages 24 & 25 Ordering a drink in a bar and in a café

2 • Ich möchte **ein Glas Rotwein**, bitte.
 • **Ein Mineralwasser**, bitte.
 • **Ein Bier**, bitte.
 • Ich möchte **eine Cola**.

3 • Guten Tag! Bitte schön?
 • Ein **Mineralwasser**, bitte.
 • Ein **Bier**, bitte.
 • Und Sie?
 • Eine **Cola**, bitte.
 • Ein **Glas Rotwein** … nein, ein **Glas Weißwein**, bitte.
 Helen: mineral water; Georg: beer; Irene: coke; Peter: glass of white wine

5 • Eine Tasse Tee mit Milch, bitte.
 • Ein Kännchen Kaffee mit Sahne, bitte.
 • Ein Kännchen Tee mit Milch, bitte.
 • Eine Tasse Kaffee ohne Milch, bitte.
 • Eine Schokolade, bitte.
 • Ein Kännchen Tee, bitte.

6 Ein Kännchen Tee mit Milch, bitte; Ein Kännchen Kaffee, bitte; Eine Tasse Tee ohne Milch, bitte; Zwei Tassen Kaffee mit Sahne, bitte.

Pages 26 & 27 Offering someone a drink and accepting or refusing

2 • Maria, was **möchten** Sie?
 • Oh, ein **Glas** Wein, bitte.
 • Ein Glas **Weißwein**?
 • Nein, **Rotwein, bitte**.
 • Und **für** Sie, Franz? **Noch** einen Kaffee?

3 Möchten Sie einen Kaffee?; Möchten Sie ein Glas Bier?; Möchten Sie eine Tasse Tee mit Milch?; Möchten Sie noch einen Kaffee?; Möchten Sie eine Cola?

5 • Barbara, möchten Sie ein Bier?
 • Gern.
 • Manfred, möchten Sie ein Glas Wein?
 • Nein, danke.

• Irene, was möchten Sie?
• Für mich nichts, danke.
• Angelika, möchten Sie einen Kaffee?
• Ja, danke.
• Franz, möchten Sie ein Glas Rotwein?
• Ja, gern … danke schön … Prost!
Barbara, Angelika and Franz accept.

6 *c* is Georg's bill.

7 Prost!; Danke schön.

Page 28 Put it all together

1 *Irene* Drei Glas Weißwein und ein Bier, bitte.
 Mann Drei Bier, eine Cola und ein Mineralwasser, bitte.

2 1 b; 2 c; 3 a; 4 c.

3 *Jutta* Ich **möchte einen** Kaffee, bitte. Und für **Sie**, Liesl?
 Liesl Für **mich** ein Bier.
 Manfred Für mich **nichts, danke**.
 Jutta Gut. Ein Bier und einen Kaffee, **bitte**.
 Jutta **Nein**, danke.

Page 29 Now you're talking!

1 • Möchten Sie einen Kaffee?
 • **Ja, gern.**
 • Mit oder ohne Sahne?
 • **Mit Sahne, bitte.**
 • **Was möchten Sie, Franz?**
 • Ein Mineralwasser, bitte.
 • **Irene, möchten Sie noch einen Kaffee?**
 • Ja, danke.
 • **Ein Mineralwasser, eine Tasse Kaffee und ein Kännchen Tee, bitte.**

2 • Bitte schön?
 • **Eine Tasse Tee mit Milch und zwei Kännchen Kaffee, bitte.**
 • Bitte schön?
 • **Ein Glas Weißwein, zwei Glas Cola und vier Bier, bitte.**

3 • Bitte schön?
• **Möchten Sie ein Bier?**
• Ja, gern.
• **Dieter, was möchten Sie?**
• Für mich ein Glas Bier.
• **Und Sie, Kerstin?**
• Für mich ein Glas Rotwein.
• **Zwei Glas Bier, ein Glas Rotwein und ein Glas Weißwein, bitte.**
• Sonst noch etwas?
• **Nein, danke.**
• Danke ... Prost!

Page 30 **Quiz**

1 white; 2 Rotwein; 3 accepting;
4 three more beers; 5 do you want anything else? 6 Bier, Wein; 7 Kaffee;
8 ein Kännchen

Unit 4 **Darf ich vorstellen?**

Page 32 **Introducing someone**

2 *a* • Darf ich **vorstellen?** Das **ist** mein Mann, Karl Fischer.
• Freut mich. Mein Name ist Joachim Schneider.
b • **Darf** ich vorstellen? Das **sind** meine Freunde, Bob und Joan Butler.
• Es freut mich, Herr Butler, Frau Butler.
• **Ebenfalls.**

3 *Liesl* Darf ich vorstellen? **Das ist mein Mann.**
Hans **Darf ich vorstellen? Das ist meine Frau.**

Page 33 **Talking about family**

2 • Sind Sie verheiratet, Brigitte?
• **Ja, ich bin verheiratet.**
• Sind Sie verheiratet, Herr Koch?
• Nein, ich bin nicht verheiratet.
• Und Sie, Frau Schwarz, sind Sie verheiratet?
• Nein, ich bin nicht verheiratet.
Brigitte is married.

4 • Frau Fischer, sind Sie verheiratet?
• Ja, ich bin verheiratet.
• Haben Sie Kinder?
• Ja, ich habe einen Sohn.
• Und Sie, Herr Schneider, sind Sie verheiratet?
• Ja, und ich habe eine Tochter und einen Sohn.
• Und Sie, Herr Müller?
• Ich bin nicht verheiratet und ich habe keine Kinder.
Irene: verheiratet; 1 Sohn
Joachim: verheiratet; 1 Tochter, 1 Sohn
Georg: nicht verheiratet; –

Page 34 **Asking and giving someone's age**

3 • Mein Sohn **Fritz ist siebzehn** und meine Tochter **Maria ist zwölf.**
• Ich habe zwei Töchter: **Liesl ist fünfzehn** und **Jutta ist dreizehn.**
Fritz: 17; Maria: 12; Liesl: 15; Jutta: 13

4 Mein Sohn Manfred **ist neunzehn.**
Meine **Tochter Angelika ist sechzehn.**
Mein Sohn Daniel ist elf.

Page 35 **Using the numbers up to 100**

2 **sechs**undzwanzig, siebenund**zwanzig**, **acht**undzwanzig, neun**undzwanzig**

4 **drei**undvierzig; **fünf**undvierzig; sechsund**vierzig**; siebenund**vierzig**; **neunundvierzig**

5 *a* Meine Frau ist **zweiunddreißig.**
b Mein Sohn Michael ist **fünfzehn.**
c Mein Mann ist **vierundsechzig.**
d Meine Tochter ist **siebzehn.**
e Meine Frau ist **neunundvierzig.**
a 32; b 15; c 64; d 17; e 49

Page 36 **Put it all together**

1 Darf ich vorstellen? Mein Name ist Jack Bradshaw. Ich bin verheiratet und habe einen Sohn und eine Tochter. Ich bin achtundvierzig Jahre alt, meine Frau

Mary ist siebenundvierzig. Mein Sohn
Frank ist sechsundzwanzig und meine
Tochter Julia ist vierundzwanzig.

2 d, b, f, e, a, c

3 Familie Schröder: 48; Familie Lindemann:
49; Familie Martens: 51; Familie Förster:
52

Page 37 **Now you're talking!**

1 ● Wie heißen Sie?
● **Ich heiße Robert Blythe.**
● Sind Sie verheiratet?
= **Ja, ich bin verheiratet. Meine
Frau heißt Clare.**
● Und haben Sie Kinder?
● **Ja, ich habe eine Tochter, Jenny.**
● Haben Sie einen Sohn?
● **Nein.**
● Wie alt ist Jenny?
● **Sie ist elf.**

2 ● Darf ich vorstellen? Das sind meine
Freunde, Stephanie und Georg Krumm
. . . Herr Blythe.
● Freut mich, Herr Blythe.
● **Ebenfalls, Frau Krumm.**
● **Das ist meine Frau, Clare ... Herr
und Frau Krumm.**
● Freut mich, Frau Blythe.

3 ● **Haben Sie Kinder?**
● Ja, ich habe einen Sohn.
● **Wie alt ist er?**
● Er ist vierzehn.

Page 38 **Quiz**
1 Das ist mein Mann; *2* Ebenfalls;
3 They haven't any children; *4* Ich bin ...
Jahre alt; *5* 18; *6* sie; *7* married;
8 Ich habe drei Söhne.

Kontrollpunkt I (Pages 39–42)

1 *a* Ja, einen Sohn; *b* Prost!; *c* Nein, danke;
d Guten Abend!; *e* Sind Sie verheiratet?;
f Gute Nacht; *g* Aus England.

2 ● Guten Abend. Ich heiße Detlev. Wie
heißen Sie?
● Mein Name ist Sylvia. Ich bin
Italienerin. Woher kommen Sie?
● Ich wohne in Wunstdorf in
Deutschland. Ich bin Mechaniker.
● Ich bin Sekretärin.
● Sind Sie verheiratet?
● Nein. Und Sie?
● Ja, ich bin verheiratet.
● Haben Sie Kinder?
● Ja, zwei Töchter. Annaliese ist
einundzwanzig und Lore ist achtzehn.
*Detlev: German; mechanic; married,
2 daughters*
Sylvia: Italian; secretary; unmarried

3 ● Wie heißen Sie, bitte?
● Mein Name ist Miller, Margaret
Miller.
● Sind Sie Engländerin, Frau Miller?
● Nein, ich komme **aus Australien.**
● Und was sind Sie?
● Ich bin **Lehrerin.**
● Und wie alt sind Sie, bitte?
● Ich bin **fünfunddreißig.**
● Sind Sie verheiratet, Frau Miller?
● Ja, und ich habe **eine Tochter.**
● Und wie heißen Sie?
● Ich heiße Steven Carter.
● Woher kommen Sie, Herr Carter?
● Ich komme **aus Hull in England.**
● Und was sind Sie?
● Ich bin **Polizist.**
● Sind Sie verheiratet, Herr Carter?
● Ja.
● Und haben Sie Kinder?
● Nein, ich habe **keine Kinder.**
● Und wie alt sind Sie?
● **Zweiunddreißig.**
Errors: Kanadierin → *Australierin;
Polizistin* → *Lehrerin; einen Sohn* → *eine
Tochter; Lehrer* → *Polizist; 42* → *32*

4 ● Brigitte, was möchten Sie?
● Oh, **ein Glas Weißwein**, bitte.
● Gut. Ach, Frau Fischer und Herr
Müller! Guten Abend!
● Guten Abend!
● Was möchten Sie?
● Für mich **Tee**, bitte.

- Mit Milch?
- Ja, mit Milch.
- Und für Sie, Herr Müller?
- **Ein Bier**, bitte.
- Ein Glas Weißwein, ein Kännchen Tee mit Milch und zwei Bier, bitte.

Brigitte: glass of white wine; Irene: pot of tea with milk; Georg: beer; Joachim: beer

5 *a* einundsiebzig, zwölf, neunundachtzig, fünfundvierzig, vierundfünfzig
b Meine Telefonnummer ist eins, sieben, acht, zwo, fünf, drei. *(178253)*

6 *a* Wie heißen Sie? *b* Wie alt sind Sie? *c* Sind Sie verheiratet? *d* Was sind Sie?

7 ● Bitte schön?
● Eine Tasse Kaffee, eine Limonade, ein Bier, ein Glas Rotwein und ein Glas Weißwein, bitte.

8 Missing words: **heiße**; Deut**schland**; **alt**; Program**mierer**; **Studen**tin; verhe**iratet**; **kommt**; **arbeits**los; Leh**rerin**
a Susi is a student and Jochen is unemployed; *b* His father is a computer programmer and his mother is a secretary; *c* 14; *d* Italian

9 *a* GUTEN MORGEN; *b* AUF WIEDERSEHEN; *c* TSCHUS; *d* MEIN NAME IST; *e* FREUT MICH; *f* GRUSS GOTT; *g* DANKE; *h* ICH BIN; *i* GUTEN ABEND; *j* WIE GEHT ES IHNEN

Unit 5 **Wo ist die Bank?**

Pages 44 & 45 Enquiring about places in town and understanding where they are

2 ● Entschuldigen Sie, wo ist **die Post**?
● Wo ist **der Bahnhof**, bitte? Ist das weit von hier?
● Wo ist **das Rathaus**, bitte?
● Ist das **der Marktplatz**?
● Entschuldigen Sie, ist das **die Bank**?

3 *a* Entschuldigen Sie, **wo ist** der Bahnhof, bitte?
b Wo ist der Dom? Ist das **weit** von hier?
c Wo ist **die Bank**, bitte?
d **Entschuldigen** Sie, ist das das Verkehrs**amt**?
e Ist das Einkaufszentrum weit **von hier**?

5 *a* ● Wo ist der Bahnhof, Brigitte?
● Wir sind hier … und der Bahnhof ist da drüben.
b ● Ach ja, und da ist die Post auch links.
c ● Gut. Und wo ist das Einkaufszentrum?
● Das Einkaufszentrum? Rechts.
d ● Danke, und wo ist die Apotheke?
● Die Apotheke ist geradeaus.
● Ist das weit von hier?
● Nein, vielleicht zehn Minuten zu Fuß.
e ● Und der Dom ist hier rechts.
a Bahnhof, O; b Post, L; c Einkaufszentrum, R; d Apotheke, S; e Dom, R

6 1 der Bahnhof; 2 das Verkehrsamt; 3 das Rathaus; 4 der Dom; 5 die Apotheke

7 Wo ist der Bahnhof?; Wo ist das Verkehrsamt?; Wo ist der Dom?

Page 46 **Following simple directions**

2 *a* ● Der Dom? Gehen Sie geradeaus und dann **links**.
b ● Wo ist das Verkehrsamt, bitte?
● Da drüben, neben der Bank.
c ● Wo ist der Bahnhof, bitte?
● Gehen Sie hier links.
d ● Wo ist das Einkaufszentrum, bitte?
● Gehen Sie rechts um die Ecke.
e ● Ist der Dom gegenüber der Bank?
● Nein, **gegenüber dem Rathaus**.
f ● Wo ist die Apotheke, bitte?
● Nehmen Sie die zweite Straße **links** und die Apotheke ist neben der Post.

3 *a* Das Museum ist neben **dem** Bahnhof.
b Der Parkplatz ist nicht weit von **der** Bank.

c Die Post ist gegenüber **dem** Einkaufszentrum.
d Der Dom ist neben **dem** Marktplatz.

Page 47 **Asking for help with understanding**

2 • Entschuldigen Sie, ich bin fremd hier. Wo ist das Rathaus?
  • Gehen Sie hier geradeaus.
  • Entschuldigen Sie, wo ist der Dom?
  • Gehen Sie hier links, nehmen Sie die zweite Straße rechts, dann geradeaus …
  • Bitte wiederholen Sie, ich verstehe nicht.
  • Entschuldigen Sie, wo ist das Verkehrsamt?
  • Hier rechts, dann geradeaus, vielleicht fünf Minuten, dann links …
  • Sprechen Sie langsamer, bitte.
  • Entschuldigen Sie, ich bin fremd hier. Wo ist die Post?
  • Um die Ecke, gegenüber dem Einkaufszentrum.
  • Ach, das Einkaufszentrum ist auch um die Ecke?
  Irene: town hall; stranger here
  Anna: cathedral; doesn't understand, please repeat
  Maria: tourist office; too fast, speak more slowly
  Jutta: post office; stranger here

3 *a* Sprechen Sie langsamer, bitte (Ich verstehe nicht); *b* Ich bin fremd hier; *c* Bitte wiederholen Sie (Ich verstehe nicht); *d* Ich verstehe nicht.

Page 48 **Put it all together**

1 Wo ist … *a* die Bank? *b* die Apotheke? *c* das Rathaus? *d* der Bahnhof? *e* der Dom? *f* das Verkehrsamt?

2 *a* das Einkaufszentrum; *b* das Verkehrsamt; *c* die Apotheke; *d* der Marktplatz

3 *a* Gehen Sie geradeaus. Das Museum ist da rechts.
  b (Gehen Sie geradeaus,) nehmen Sie die zweite Straße links. Die Bank ist da rechts.

Page 49 **Now you're talking!**

1 • **Guten Morgen. Wo ist der Dom, bitte?**
  • Der Dom? Der Dom ist neben dem Rathaus.
  • **Ist das weit?**
  • Nein, zehn Minuten zu Fuß.
  • **Und wo ist die Bank?**
  • Gegenüber dem Rathaus.
  • **Danke. Auf Wiedersehen.**

2 • **Entschuldigen Sie, wo ist das Einkaufszentrum?**
  • Das ist nicht weit – geradeaus, die zweite Straße rechts und da ist es.
  • **Bitte wiederholen Sie.**
  • Das ist nicht weit – immer geradeaus, die zweite Straße rechts und da ist es.
  • **Ich verstehe nicht. Sprechen Sie langsamer, bitte.**

3 • **Entschuldigen Sie, ich bin fremd hier.**
  • Ja?
  • **Wo ist das Verkehrsamt, bitte?**
  • Gehen Sie rechts um die Ecke.
  • **Danke. Auf Wiedersehen.**

4 • **Gehen Sie geradeaus. Nehmen Sie die erste Straße rechts. Der Dom ist links neben dem Rathaus.**

Page 50 **Quiz**

1 The shopping centre is over there; *2* Wo ist die Apotheke?; *3* Ich verstehe nicht; *4* Go straight ahead; *5* Take the second road on the left; *6* When someone speaks too fast; *7* neben; *8* Verkehrsbüro

Unit 6 **Haben Sie Orangen?**

Pages 52 & 53 **Asking for what you want and understanding the assistant**

2 *a* Was kosten die Orangen, bitte?
  b Haben Sie Bananen?
  c Eine Ananas und drei Orangen, bitte.

a oranges; b bananas; c a pineapple and three oranges

3 • Bitte schön?
  • Was **kosten** die Bananen?
  • Vier Bananen kosten einen Euro fünfzig.
  • Und **haben** Sie Orangen?
  • Ja, hier. Eine Orange **kostet** dreißig Cent.
  • Ich möchte sechs.
  • Sonst noch etwas?
  • Ja, was **kostet** eine Ananas?
  • Zwei Euro fünfzig.
  • Gut. Vier Bananen, sechs Orangen und eine Ananas, bitte.

5 *a* • Guten Tag. **Kann ich Ihnen helfen?**
  • Ja, ich möchte sechs Tomaten, bitte.
  • Sechs Tomaten kosten einen Euro vierzig. Sonst noch etwas?
  • Ja, und die Trauben.
  • **Die hier?** Gut. Sie kosten drei Euro zwanzig **das Kilo.**
  • Danke.
  b • Guten Tag.
  • Guten Tag. Ich möchte Brötchen, bitte. Was kosten sie?
  • Dreißig Cent **das Stück.**
  • Ich möchte zehn, bitte.

6 € 1,40; € 3,20; Ct. 30; total € 4,90

Page 54 Buying the quantity you want

2 *a* zweihundertfünfzig Gramm Trauben (*250 g*); *b* ein halber Liter Milch (¹/₂ *l*); *c* ein Liter Rotwein (*1 l*); *d* und ein halbes Kilo Tomaten (¹/₂ *kg*).

3 • Guten Morgen. Ich möchte **eine Flasche Orangensaft**, bitte.
  • Kann ich Ihnen helfen?
  • Ja, **eine Dose Tomaten**, bitte.
  • Ich möchte **ein Päckchen Kekse.**
  • Ich möchte **eine Packung Apfelsaft**, bitte.

4 Eine **Flasche** Orangensaft, ein halbes Kilo **Bananen**, ein Liter **Mineralwasser**, ein

Päckchen Kaffee, sechs **Brötchen**, eine **Dose** Cola, eine Packung **Milch** und **hundert Gramm** Tee.

Page 55 Dealing with money

2 • Entschuldigen Sie. Wo kann ich **Geld wechseln?**
  • In der Bank um die Ecke.
  • Das macht € 49, bitte.
  • Kann ich Ihnen helfen?
  • Ja, ich möchte diesen **Reisescheck einlösen.**
  • Kann ich **mit Kreditkarte bezahlen?**
  • Mit Kreditkarte? Ja, kein Problem!
  Manfred: change money; Georg: cash a traveller's cheque; Maria: pay by credit card

3 *a* wechseln; *b* einlösen; *c* einlösen

Page 56 Put it all together

1 Trauben: 250 g; Apfelsaft: Flasche/ 1 Liter; Kekse: Päckchen; Wein: Flasche/1 Liter; Cola: Flasche/Dose

2 eine Flasche Orangensaft; ein Liter Rotwein; ein halbes Kilo Tomaten; vier Bananen; eine Dose Tomaten; ein Päckchen Kekse; sechs Brötchen

3 *a* Was kosten die Orangen?
  b Ich möchte diesen Reisescheck einlösen.
  c Wo kann ich Geld wechseln?
  d Kann ich Ihnen helfen?
  e Was kostet eine Ananas?
  f Kann ich mit Kreditkarte bezahlen?

Page 57 Now you're talking!

1 • Tag. Kann ich Ihnen helfen?
  • **Guten Tag. Zweihundertfünfzig Gramm Trauben und ein Kilo Bananen, bitte.**
  • Sonst noch etwas?
  • **Ich möchte ein halbes Kilo Tomaten.**
  • Gut. Und sonst noch etwas?

● **Nein, das ist alles. Danke schön.**

2   ● **Ich möchte sechs Brötchen,
        bitte.**
     ● Sonst noch etwas?
     ● **Was kostet ein Päckchen Kekse?**
     ● Einen Euro fünfzig das Päckchen.
     ● **Ich möchte ein Päckchen und
        eine Flasche Rotwein.**
     ● Sonst noch etwas?
     ● **Ja, ich möchte einen Liter
        Apfelsaft.**
     ● Gut. Zehn Euro achtzig, bitte.

3   ● **Guten Tag. Ich möchte Geld
        wechseln.**
     ● Ja, gut … das sind dann
        zweihundertfünfzehn Euro.
     ● **Danke. Auf Wiedersehen.**

Page 58 **Quiz**

1a Was kosten? *b* Was kostet? *c* Was
kostet?; 2 Haben Sie Tomaten?; *3* 100;
4 Ein Tomatenbrötchen, bitte;
5 einlösen; 6 $^1/_4$ litre; 7 10 oranges;
8 Packung

Unit 7 **Wo finde ich Geschenke?**

**Pages 60 & 61 Finding the right
department in a department store**

2   *a* die Schreibwarenabteilung;
     b die Haushaltswarenabteilung;
     c die Lederwarenabteilung

3   ● Entschuldigen Sie. Wo finde ich die
        Sportabteilung?
     ● Die Sportabteilung ist im zweiten
        Stock.
     ● Wo finde ich Süßwaren?
     ● Im dritten Stock.
     ● Wo finde ich Lederwaren, bitte?
     ● Die Lederwarenabteilung ist im
        ersten Stock.
     *sports department – second floor; leather
     goods – first floor; confectionery –
     third floor*

5   *a* Der Parkplatz ist im Erdgeschoss.
     b Die Toiletten sind auch im
        Erdgeschoss.
     c Das Restaurant? Das ist im dritten
        Stock.
     a richtig; b falsch; c falsch

6   a ● Entschuldigen Sie. Wo **sind** die
          Toiletten?
       ● Die Toiletten? Sie sind **im
          Erdgeschoss**, neben dem
          Parkplatz.
     b ● Wo **ist** das Restaurant?
       ● Gegenüber der Bank **im dritten
          Stock**.
     c ● Wo finde ich Geschenke?
       ● Die Geschenkabteilung ist **im
          Untergeschoss**.

Page 62 **Getting just what you want**

2   *a* ● Ich möchte **Pralinen**, bitte.
       ● Die Pralinen hier?
       ● Ja, die sind **schön**.
     b ● Was kostet eine **Flasche Wein**?
       ● Diese Flasche kostet vierunddreißig
          Euro.
       ● Oh, das ist **zu teuer**.
     c ● Ich suche **eine Tasche**, aber die
          Tasche hier ist **zu groß**.
       ● Möchten Sie vielleicht die Tasche da?
     *a chocolates, nice; b bottle of wine, too
     expensive; c handbag, too big*

3   ● Ich suche ein T-Shirt.
     ● Das T-Shirt hier ist schön.
     ● Ja, aber das ist zu klein.
     ● Ich suche eine Flasche Rotwein. Was
        kostet diese Flasche?
     ● Zwei Euro sechzig.
     ● Ja, gut.
     ● Was kostet die Tasche, bitte?
     ● Fünf Euro fünfundvierzig.
     ● Öh, das ist nicht teuer.
     ● Haben Sie Pralinen?
     ● Ja, die hier kosten vierzehn Euro
        fünfzig.
     ● Oh, die sind zu teuer!
     Kerstin may buy the wine and the bag.

4 Das ist zu groß; Ich nehme eine Flasche Wein; Ich suche eine Tasche.

Page 63 Understanding opening times

2 Store *b* is open Monday–Friday.

3 *a* Wir sind von neun bis sechs geöffnet. Dienstag ist Ruhetag.
   b Wir sind von acht bis zwölf und von zwei bis sechs geöffnet. Wir sind montags geschlossen.
   c Wir sind von neun bis eins und von zwei bis sieben geöffnet. Donnerstag ist Ruhetag.
   a 9 a.m.–6 p.m., closed Tuesdays; *b* 8–12 a.m. & 2–6 p.m., closed Mondays; *c* 9 a.m. –1 p.m. & 2–7 p.m., closed Thursdays

Page 64 Put it all together

1 *a* Tuesday rest day; *b* toilets in the basement; *c* open from 8 to 12 and from 2 to 7; *d* restaurant closed until Thursday

2 *b, d, e, c, a*

3 *a* expensive; *b* big; *c* nice; *d* small

4 *a* Lederwarenabteilung;
   b Süßwarenabteilung;
   c Lebensmittelabteilung;
   d Haushaltswarenabteilung

Page 65 Now you're talking!

1 • **Entschuldigen Sie. Wo sind die Toiletten?**
   • Die Toiletten sind im zweiten Stock.
   • **Danke. Wo finde ich die Sportabteilung?**
   • Im Erdgeschoss.
   • **Ist das neben der Lebensmittelabteilung?**
   • Ja, neben der Lebensmittelabteilung.
2 • **Ich suche Geschenke.**
   • Vielleicht Pralinen?
   • **Die sind zu teuer.**
   • Eine Tasche? Oder eine Flasche

Wein?
   • **Was kostet eine Tasche?**
   • Fünfundzwanzig Euro.
   • **Gut. Ich nehme eine Tasche.**

3 • **Wann sind Sie geöffnet?**
   • Wir sind von neun bis sechs geöffnet. Montag ist Ruhetag.
   • **Wo ist der Parkplatz?**
   • Im Untergeschoss, neben der Haushaltswarenabteilung.
   • **Danke. Auf Wiedersehen.**

Page 66 Quiz

1 Mittwoch; 2 geöffnet;
3 im Restaurant; 4 We're closed on Wednesdays; 5 Samstag, Sonnabend;
6 Untergeschoss; 7 the T-shirt;
8 in der Schreibwarenabteilung

Kontrollpunkt 2 (Pages 67–70)

1 *a* the chemist's; *b* the station;
   c first road on the right; *d* the tourist information office; *e* straight ahead;
   f on the third floor; *g* the restaurant;
   h opposite; *i* left; *j* in the stationery department

2 1 COLA; 2 KAFFEE; 3 KEKSE;
   4 ANANAS; 5 ORANGEN;
   6 APFELSAFT; 7 FLASCHE;
   8 BANANEN; 9 DOSE; 10 WEIN;
   11 TOMATEN; 12 TRAUBEN

3 **eine** Ananas; **sechs Dosen** Cola;
   ein halbes Kilo Trauben;
   ein Päckchen Kaffee; **fünf** Orangen;
   eine Flasche Weißwein

4 *a* • Was kostet der Wein?
     • Sieben Euro.
   b • Die Tasche kostet **siebenund-sechzig Euro fünfzig**? Oh, das ist teuer!
   c • Das kostet **zwei Euro dreißig**. Gut!
   d • Was kosten die Pralinen?
     • Vierzehn Euro zwanzig.

e • Die kosten **vierzig Euro.**
f • Was kostet das T-Shirt?
  • Vier Euro fünfzig.
  • Gut, ich nehme das T-Shirt.
g • Das kostet sechsundvierzig Euro?
  Nein, das ist zu teuer!
  b € 67,50; c € 2,30; e € 40,00

5 a • Ich möchte **drei Bananen, eine
    Ananas** und **ein halbes Kilo
    Tomaten.**
  • **Sechs Euro fünfundsiebzig
    (€ 6,75),** bitte.
  b • Ich möchte **eine Flasche
    Limonade, ein Karton Milch** und
    ein Päckchen Kaffee.
  • **Elf Euro fünfzehn (€ 11,15),** bitte.

6 a Gehen Sie hier rechts und nehmen
    Sie die dritte Straße links. Das ist
    dann links.
  b Gehen Sie geradeaus. Nehmen Sie die
    zweite Straße links und dann die erste
    Straße links und dann ist es rechts.
  c Gehen Sie geradeaus. Nehmen Sie die
    zweite Straße rechts und dann die
    erste Straße links. Das ist dann rechts.
  *a shopping centre; b tourist office;
  c cathedral*

7 *a* 1st; *b* 2nd; *c* 3rd; *d* ground floor;
  e basement

8 *a* der Sportabteilung; *b* dem Restaurant;
  c sind neben

9 *c* False: she has an office on the 2nd
    floor.
  d False: he has an hour.
  f False: it's not far.

Unit 8 **Ich möchte ein Zimmer**

Page 72 Checking in at reception

2 • Guten Tag. Ich heiße Friedmann,
    Martin Friedmann.
  • Guten Tag, Herr Friedmann. Ein
    Einzelzimmer mit **Bad,** nicht wahr?
    Zimmer Nummer siebenunddreißig

(**37**). Hier ist der Schlüssel.
  • Guten Abend. Ich habe eine
    Reservierung für ein Doppelzimmer.
    Mein Name ist Doris Wolf.
  • Ein **Doppelzimmer** mit **Dusche,**
    Frau Wolf, ja? ... Hier ist der
    Schlüssel, Nummer hundertzwanzig
    (**120**).
  • Guten Abend. Wie heißen Sie, bitte?
  • Lange, Michael Lange. Ich habe eine
    Reservierung für ein Einzelzimmer.
  • Oh ja, ein **Einzelzimmer** mit **Bad.**
    Zimmer Nummer vierundsechzig (**64**).

3 a • Guten Tag. Ich heiße Anna
    Dürnbeck.
  • Ach ja, ein **Einzelzimmer,** nicht
    wahr? Nummer fünfzig im **zweiten**
    Stock. Hier ist der Schlüssel.
  b • Guten Abend. Mein Name ist Fritz
    Auerbach. Ich habe eine
    Reservierung für ein Doppelzimmer
    im **Erdgeschoss.**
  • Oh ja, Herr Auerbach, ein
    Doppelzimmer mit Bad.
  c • Guten Abend. Ich habe eine
    Reservierung für **ein
    Einzelzimmer mit Dusche.**
  • Wie heißen Sie, bitte?
  • Meyer, Heinrich.
  • Ja, Zimmer hundertvierzehn im
    ersten Stock.
  Heinrich Meyer (c) was asked his name.

Page 73 **Asking for a hotel room**

2 a • Guten Tag. Haben Sie ein Zimmer
    frei?
  • Möchten Sie ein Einzelzimmer oder
    ein Doppelzimmer?
  • Ein Einzelzimmer mit Dusche **für
    zwei Nächte,** bitte.
  b • Guten Abend. Haben Sie ein
    Doppelzimmer frei?
  • Für wie lange?
  • **Für drei Nächte.**
  c • Guten Abend. Haben Sie ein
    Zimmer frei?
  • Für heute oder ...?
  • Ja, **für heute.** Ein Einzelzimmer,
    bitte.

a 2 nights; b 3 nights; c tonight

3   A, B, C, D, E, F, G, H, I, J, K, L, M, N,
    O, P, Q, R, S, T, U, V, W, X, Y, Z
    Ä, Ö, Ü
    KURT STOCKER
    Familienname: Stocker

4   *a* ● Wie heißen Sie, bitte?
       ● Henkel, Martha.
       ● Henkel, wie schreibt man das?
       ● **HENKEL.**
       ● Und Martha?
       ● **MARTHA.**

    b ● Guten Tag, ich habe eine
          Reservierung.
       ● Wie heißen Sie, bitte?
       ● Anja Weidmann.
       ● Wie schreibt man das?
       ● **WEIDMANN.**
       ● Und Anja?
       ● **ANJA.**
       ● Danke. Hier ist der Schlüssel.

    c ● Wie heißen Sie?
       ● Mein Familienname ist Schmid.
       ● **SCHMID.**
       ● Und der Vorname?
       ● Oskar.
       ● **OSKAR.**
       ● Ist gut, Herr Schmid. Danke.

5   Haben Sie ein Zimmer frei für heute?;
    Ein Einzelzimmer für vier Nächte, bitte;
    Haben Sie ein Doppelzimmer (frei) für
    drei Nächte?

Page 74 Booking ahead

2   *a* ● Hotel Sonne, guten Abend.
       ● Guten Abend. Ich möchte ein
         Doppelzimmer reservieren.
       ● Für wann?
       ● **Vom neunundzwanzigsten Juni
         bis zum zwölften Juli.**
       ● Ja, mit Bad oder mit Dusche?

    b ● Guten Tag. Hotel Sonne.
       ● Guten Tag. Ich möchte ein
         Einzelzimmer **vom fünften bis
         zum achten März** reservieren.

● Es tut mir leid, das Hotel ist voll
  besetzt.
c ● Guten Tag. Hotel Sonne.
   ● Guten Tag. Haben Sie ein
     Doppelzimmer mit Dusche frei?
   ● Für wann?
   ● **Vom zweiten April bis zum
     vierten Mai.**
   ● Ja, wie heißen Sie, bitte?
a 29/6–12/7; b 5–8/3; c 2/4–4/5;
customer b will be disappointed

Page 75 Enquiring about facilities

2/3 *a* ● Wann ist Frühstück, bitte?
       ● Von sieben bis neun.
     b ● Bis wann ist die Bar geöffnet?
       ● Die Bar? Bis elf Uhr.
     c ● Gibt es ein Schwimmbad hier im
         Hotel?
       ● Nein, es tut mir leid. Es gibt ein
         Schwimmbad in der Nähe, neben
         dem Rathaus.
     d ● Gibt es einen Parkplatz?
       ● Ja, es gibt einen Parkplatz hinter
         dem Hotel.
*a When is breakfast? From 7 till 9; b Until
when is the bar open? Until 11; c Is there
a swimming pool in the hotel? No, but
there's one nearby, next to the town hall;
d Is there a car park? Yes, behind the hotel.*

4   ● Hier ist das Hotel Sonne. Wir haben
      Zimmer **für drei Nächte.**
    ● Wann ist Frühstück?
    ● Frühstück ist **von sechs bis zehn**
      und das Restaurant ist abends **von
      sieben bis elf** geöffnet. Es gibt eine
      Bar **neben dem Restaurant im
      Erdgeschoss.**
    ● Bis wann ist die Bar geöffnet?
    ● Die Bar ist auch bis elf Uhr abends
      geöffnet.
    ● Gibt es ein Schwimmbad?
    ● Ja, es gibt ein Schwimmbad **im
      Untergeschoss.**
*a from 6 to 10 o'clock; b from 7 to 11 p.m.;
c ground floor, next to restaurant;
d basement; They will be staying for 3
nights.*

Page 76 **Put it all together**

1 Familienname: Kraus Vorname: Hans
   Beruf: Architekt Nationalität:
   Holländer
   Zimmernummer: 76 vom 11/9 bis
   zum 18/9

2 *a* ein Einzelzimmer mit Dusche; *b* einen
   Parkplatz; *c* Frühstück; *d* ersten bis zum
   vierten März

3 *a* When for?; *b* Have you a room?;
   c The hotel's full; *d* nearby; *e* behind the
   hotel; *f* For how long?

Page 77 **Now you're talking!**

1 ● Guten Tag. Kann ich Ihnen helfen?
   ● **Guten Tag. Haben Sie ein**
     Zimmer frei?
   ● Ein Einzelzimmer oder ein
     Doppelzimmer?
   ● **Ein Einzelzimmer mit Bad.**
   ● Für wie lange?
   ● **Für drei Nächte.**
   ● Gut. Also Zimmer dreiundneunzig im
     zweiten Stock.

2 ● **Guten Tag. Ich habe eine**
     Reservierung.
   ● Wie heißen Sie?
   ● **Ich heiße James Wilson.**
   ● Ein Doppelzimmer mit Dusche, nicht
     wahr?
   ● **Ja, vom neunzehnten bis zum**
     sechsundzwanzigsten Juni.
   ● Gut. Hier ist der Schlüssel, Herr
     Wilson.
   ● **Gibt es einen Parkplatz in der**
     Nähe?
   ● Ja, hinter dem Hotel.

3 ● Guten Morgen. Eurotel Dresden.
   ● **Guten Morgen. Ich möchte ein**
     Zimmer reservieren.
   ● Für wann?
   ● **Für heute.**
   ● Für wie lange?
   ● **Bis zum zwölften.**
   ● Ja, wie heißen Sie, bitte?

● **Ich heiße + *your name*.**
● Wie schreibt man das?
● **Spell your name.**

Page 78 **Quiz**

1 März; *2* 3rd to 9th May; *3* What
time is breakfast?; *4* Gibt es ein
Schwimmbad in der Nähe?;
5 Familienname; *6* five nights; *7* spell
out what you just said; *8* regret

Unit 9 **Wann fährt der nächste Zug?**

Pages 80 & 81 Asking about public
transport and arrival and departure
times

2 ● Welche Linie fährt zum Rathaus?
   ● Die Linie fünf.
   ● Welche Linie fährt zur Stadtmitte?
   ● Die Linie siebenundzwanzig.
   ● Welche Linie fährt nach Schwabing?
   ● Die Linie vierzehn.
   ● Welche Linie fährt zum Bahnhof?
   ● Die Linie zweiunddreißig oder die
     Linie acht.
   a 5, town hall; *b* 27, town centre;
   c 14, Schwabing; *d* 32 or 8, station

3 ● Fährt diese **Straßenbahn** zum
     Rathaus, bitte?
   ● Nein, **nach** Schwabing. Der Bus
     fährt zum Rathaus. Dort drüben ist
     die **Bushaltestelle.**
   ● Welche **Linie** fährt **zum** Rathaus?
   ● Die **Linie** fünf.

5 ● Der Zug nach Zürich fährt um
     siebzehn Uhr zwanzig ab.
   ● Der Intercity nach Leipzig fährt in
     zehn Minuten um acht Uhr ab.
   ● Der Zug nach Wien kommt **um**
     dreiundzwanzig Uhr vierzehn in
     Linz an.
   ● Der Zug nach Siegen kommt um
     fünfzehn Uhr dreißig an.
   Siegen: Ankunft 15:30
   Linz: Ankunft 23:14

Zürich: Abfahrt 17:20
Leipzig: Abfahrt 8:10

6 • Wann kommt der nächste Zug in
     Garmisch an?
   • Um dreizehn Uhr dreißig.
   • Wann kommt der Bus in Schwabing
     an?
   • Um siebzehn Uhr fünfzehn.
   • Wann fährt der Bus zum Stadion?
   • Um neun Uhr zwanzig.
   • Wann fährt die Straßenbahn Linie
     sechs zur Stadtmitte?
   • Um zwanzig Uhr.
   Garmisch: 13:30; train
   Schwabing: 17:15; bus
   stadium: 9:20; bus
   town centre: 20.00; tram

Pages 82 & 83 **Buying tickets and checking travel details**

2 • Einmal zweiter Klasse hin und zurück
     nach Innsbruck, bitte.
   • Dreimal erster Klasse einfach nach
     Potsdam, bitte.
   • Zweimal zweiter Klasse einfach nach
     Augsburg.
   • Einmal zweiter Klasse hin und zurück
     nach Vaduz.
   • Viermal zweiter Klasse einfach nach
     Basel, bitte.
   Innsbruck: 1; 2nd; return
   Potsdam: 3; 1st; single
   Augsburg: 2; 2nd; single
   Vaduz: 1; 2nd; return
   Basel: 4; 2nd; single

3 *a* Zweimal erster Klasse einfach nach
     München, bitte.
   b Einmal zweiter Klasse hin und zurück
     nach Innsbruck, bitte.
   c Viermal zweiter Klasse einfach nach
     Mainz, bitte.
   d Dreimal zweiter Klasse hin und
     zurück nach Mannheim, bitte.

5 *a* • Ich möchte nach Augsburg. Muss
       ich umsteigen?
     • Ja, in München.
   b • Einmal einfach nach Hamburg, bitte.

   Kann ich einen Platz reservieren?
   • Ja, sicher.
   c • Von welchem Gleis fährt der Zug
       nach Basel?
     • Von Gleis 5B.
   d • Ich möchte nach Potsdam.
       Wo muss ich aussteigen?
     • In Berlin.
   a Augsburg; Do I have to change?
   b Hamburg; Can I reserve a seat?
   *c Basel; What platform does the train go
   from?*
   e Potsdam; Where must I get off?

6 *a* Ja, in Köln; *b* Ja, sicher; *c* Von Gleis 7;
   d In Berlin.

7 Muss ich umsteigen?
   Von welchem Gleis fährt der Zug?
   Wo muss ich aussteigen?

Page 84 **Put it all together**

1 *A1* Einmal nach Bonn, bitte.
   A2 Nach Bonn? Ja, einfach oder hin und
        zurück?
   A3 Einfach, bitte.
   A4 € 28,40 einmal einfach nach Bonn.
   B1 Wann fährt der Bus zur Stadtmitte,
        bitte?
   B2 Die Linie 7 zur Stadtmitte? Um 17:00.
   B3 Und wo ist die Bushaltestelle für die
        Linie 7?
   B4 Da drüben, gegenüber dem Rathaus.

2 *a* vierzehn Uhr vierzig; *b* sechzehn Uhr
   dreißig; *c* zwölf Uhr fünf; *d* sieben Uhr
   fünfzehn

3 *a* welchem; *b* Wann; *c* Wo; *d* Welche;
   e Wo

4 *a* nach; *b* zur; *c* zum; nach

Page 85 **Now you're talking!**

1 • Der nächste Zug nach Bad Tölz fährt
     in zwanzig Minuten von Gleis vier ab.
   • **Wann fährt der nächste Zug nach
     Bad Tölz?**
   • In zwanzig Minuten, um dreizehn Uhr

fünfundzwanzig.
- **Von welchem Gleis fährt der Zug?**
- Von Gleis vier.
- **Einmal zweiter Klasse hin und zurück nach Bad Tölz, bitte.**

2 • **Einmal zweiter Klasse einfach nach Hamburg, bitte.**
- Nach Hamburg?
- **Ja, was kostet es?**
- Es kostet neunzig Euro.
- **Kann ich einen Platz reservieren?**
- Ja, sicher.

3 • **Wo ist die Bushaltestelle?**
- Gegenüber dem Rathaus.
- **Einmal hin und zurück, bitte. Was kostet es?**
- Das kostet zwölf Euro.
- **Wann fährt der nächste Bus?**
- Um zehn Uhr dreißig.
- **Wann kommt der Bus in Oberammergau an?**
- Er kommt um elf Uhr fünfzig an.
- **Wo muss ich aussteigen?**
- Am Marktplatz.
- **Ist es weit zum Stadttheater?**
- Nein, zehn Minuten zu Fuß.
- **Wann fährt der Bus nach München?**
- Der Bus fährt um ... siebzehn Uhr fünfzehn.

Page 86 **Quiz**
1 change in Koblenz; *2* at the station; *3* Linie; *4* zum Bahnhof; *5* it's going to Bonn; *6* Ankunft; *7* mit der Straßenbahn; *8* einen Platz

Unit 10 **Guten Appetit!**

Page 88 **Reading the menu**

2 • Die Speisekarte, bitte.
- Bitte schön.
- Sauerbraten ... Was für Fleisch ist das? Ist das Rindfleisch?
- Ja, das ist Rindfleisch.
- Und was ist Weißwurst?

- Weißwurst ist Kalbfleisch.
- Ist Jägerschnitzel Schweinefleisch oder Kalbfleisch?
- Jägerschnitzel ist Schweinefleisch.
Sauerbraten = beef; Weißwurst = veal; Jägerschnitzel = pork

3 *a* seafood; *b* seafood; *c* pork; *d* beef; *e* veal; *f* pork; *g* beef; *h* seafood

Page 89 **Ordering a meal**

2 • Bitte schön?
- Was **empfehlen** Sie?
- Der Sauerbraten und das Hähnchen mit Salat sind **gut**.
- Ich nehme das Hähnchen.
- Und was ist die **Tagessuppe?**
- Tomatensuppe.
- Also eine Tomatensuppe und zwei Hähnchen.
'Salat' is salad.

3 • Und zum Trinken?
- Ein Viertelliterglas Weißwein, bitte.
- Für mich eine Flasche Mineralwasser.
Helga: quarter litre glass of white wine; Kurt: bottle of mineral water

4 *a* • Bitte schön?
- Ich möchte Melone mit Schinken, bitte.
- Und dann?
- Schweinekotelett mit Salat.
b • Was empfehlen Sie?
- Die Tagessuppe ist Tomatensuppe. Der Fisch und das Rumpsteak sind gut.
- Gut. Ich nehme Fisch mit Pommes frites.
- Und die Suppe?
- Nein, danke.
c • Die Speisekarte, bitte.
- Bitte schön.
- Ich möchte Heringssalat und dann Hähnchen.
- Mit Reis oder Pommes frites?
- Mit Reis, bitte.
- ... Guten Appetit!
b; two; salad; c; rice

Page 90 **Choosing cakes and desserts**

2 • Möchten Sie eine Nachspeise?
  • Was für Nachspeisen gibt es?
  • Na, es gibt gemischtes Eis,
    Schokoladentorte, Nusstorte,
    Käsekuchen, oder wir haben auch
    frisches Obst.
  • Für mich **Käsekuchen**, bitte.
  • Als Nachspeise nehme ich frisches
    Obst … nein, nein, **gemischtes Eis**.
  • **Mit Sahne?**
  • Ja, bitte.

3 • Was möchten Sie, Claudia?
  • Ich möchte ein Stück **Nusstorte mit
    Sahne**.
  • Und Sie, Manfred?
  • Für mich **Schokoladentorte**, aber
    keine Sahne.
  • Und ich nehme ein Stück **Obsttorte**
    ohne Sahne.
  • So, **ein Stück Nusstorte mit
    Sahne, einmal Schokotorte und
    einmal Obsttorte**. Und zum
    Trinken?
  • Drei Tassen Kaffee, bitte.
  Order c

Page 91 **Finishing the meal**

2 • Die Rechnung, bitte.
  • Ja, gut. Hat's geschmeckt?
  • Ja, es hat gut geschmeckt.
  • So, eine Tomatensuppe, zwei
    Hähnchen, Schokoladentorte,
    Käsekuchen, Weißwein und
    Mineralwasser – das macht sieben-
    undzwanzig Euro dreißig. Zahlen Sie
    bitte an der Kasse.
  • Das ist für Sie.
  • Danke schön. Auf Wiedersehen.
  *a Schokoladentorte, Käsekuchen; b at the
  cash desk; c yes; d € 27,30*

3 • Die **Rechnung**, bitte.
  • Ja, gut. Hat's **geschmeckt?**
  • Ja, es hat **gut geschmeckt**.
    Was macht das?
  • Das **macht** sechsunddreißig Euro.
  • Danke. Das ist **für Sie**.
  Was macht das? = What does it come to?

4 Die Rechnung, bitte; Das ist für Sie;
   Es hat gut geschmeckt.

Page 92 **Put it all together**

I Vorspeisen: Heringssalat,
   Tomatensuppe, Tunfischsalat;
   Hauptgerichte: Schweinekotelett,
   Hähnchen, Rinderbraten, Kalbsleber;
   Nachspeisen: Käsekuchen, gemischtes
   Eis, Apfelkuchen, frisches Obst

2 I e; 2 c; 3 g; 4 a; 5 d; 6 f; 7 b

3 *a* Einen Viertelliter Weißwein, bitte;
   b Ich nehme gemischtes Eis; *c* Es hat gut
   geschmeckt; *d* € 45,20; *e* Der Fisch ist
   gut; *f* Das ist Kalbfleisch.

Page 93 **Now you're talking!**

I • **Die Speisekarte, bitte.**
   • Bitte schön.
   • **Was für Fleisch ist das?**
   • Eisbein – das ist Schweinefleisch.
   • **Ich nehme Hähnchen mit Reis.**
   • Und zum Trinken?
   • **Ein Glas Mineralwasser, bitte.**

2 • **Was empfehlen Sie?**
   • Der Fisch ist heute sehr frisch.
   • **Gut. Also der Fisch, bitte.**
   • Mit Salat oder Pommes frites?
   • **Ich möchte Salat.**

3 • Guten Appetit! … Hat's geschmeckt?
   • **Ja, es hat gut geschmeckt.
     Als Nachspeise nehme ich
     frisches Obst.**
   • Und sonst noch etwas?
   • **Ich möchte ein Kännchen Kaffee
     mit Sahne.**

4 • **Die Rechnung, bitte.**
   • Also … Fisch mit Salat, frisches Obst
     und ein Kännchen Kaffee … das
     macht dreizehn Euro sechzig. Zahlen
     Sie bitte an der Kasse.
   • **Das ist für Sie.**
   • Danke schön. Auf Wiedersehen.

Page 94 **Quiz**

1 Schweinekotelett; *2* Guten Appetit!;
3 Vorspeisen, Hauptgerichte,
Nachspeisen; *4* Wiener Schnitzel; *5* Es
hat gut geschmeckt; *6* Tomatensuppe;
7 pay; *8* when giving a tip

Kontrollpunkt 3 (Pages 95–99)

1 ● Guten Abend. Ich habe eine
 Reservierung.
 ● Wie **heißen Sie**, bitte?
 ● Mein **Name** ist (your name).
 = Ach ja, ein Einzelzimmer mit Bad,
 nicht wahr?
 ● Nein, nein, ein Einzelzimmer **mit
 Dusche.**
 ● Oh, entschuldigen Sie, und bis wann?
 ● Bis **zum neunten.**

2 ● Kann ich Ihnen helfen?
 ● **Wann ist Frühstück, bitte?**
 ● Von sieben bis zehn.
 ● Und **wo ist die Bar?**
 ● Im Erdgeschoss neben dem
 Restaurant.
 ● Danke. Und **wann ist die Bar
 geöffnet?**
 ● Von drei Uhr nachmittags bis elf Uhr
 abends.
 ● **Gibt es ein Schwimmbad im
 Hotel?**
 ● Nein, es tut mir leid, aber es gibt ein
 Schwimmbad in der Nähe neben dem
 Museum.
 a from 7 until 10; b on the ground floor
 next to the restaurant; c from 3 p.m. until
 11 p.m.; d no, but there is one nearby,
 next to the museum

3 *a* die Fähre; *b* kommt; *c* hin und zurück

4 Ich möchte Heringssalat; Hähnchen mit
 Reis, bitte; Ja, als Nachspeise nehme ich
 frisches Obst; *c* Guten Appetit!

5 Gehen Sie hier geradeaus, nehmen Sie
 die erste Straße links und dann die
 zweite Straße rechts.

6 ● Bitte schön?
 ● **Ich möchte eine Tasche. Was
 kosten sie?**
 ● Fünfundvierzig Euro (€ **45**).
 ● **Die sind zu teuer.**
 ● Die Tasche hier ist schön und kostet
 siebenundzwanzig Euro fünfzig
 (€ **27,50**).
 ● **Das ist schön. Ich nehme die
 Tasche.**
 ● Danke. Zahlen Sie bitte an der Kasse.
 ● **Kann ich mit Kreditkarte
 bezahlen?**
 ● Ja, sicher.

7 a ● **Wo wohnen Sie?**
 ● Ich wohne in Potsdam.
 b ● **Sind Sie verheiratet?**
 ● Ja, mein Mann heißt Martin.
 c ● **Haben Sie Kinder?**
 ● Ja, einen Sohn, Dieter, und eine
 Tochter, Undine.
 d ● **Wie alt ist Undine?**
 ● Sie ist fünfzehn.
 e ● **Wie alt ist Dieter?**
 ● Er ist achtzehn.
 f ● **Was sind Sie?**
 ● Ich bin Programmiererin und mein
 Mann ist Lehrer.
 g ● **Was möchten Sie?**
 ● Ein Glas Weißwein, bitte.
 h ● **Also ein Glas Weißwein und
 ein Glas Rotwein, bitte.**

8 *a* Haus Vogtland (Tuesday) and
 Rathauskeller (Monday);
 b in the market square;
 c in the old town, opposite the
 cathedral; *d* Rathauskeller;
 e Rathauskeller (Saturday and Sunday);
 f Haus Vogtland and Zum goldenen
 Löwen; *g* gloves: Lederwaren, 2nd;
 sausage: Lebensmittel, basement;
 notepaper: Schreibwaren, ground;
 chocolates: Süßwaren, ground;
 perfume: Parfum, 1st; *h* wine;
 i behind the town hall; *j* arrival at
 Neuschwanstein; *k* half an hour;
 l next to the post office

Grammar

Grammar is simply the term used to describe the structures and patterns of a language. In German these are clearly defined and familiarity with them enables you to move away from total reliance on set phrases.

1   **Nouns** (words for people, things, places, concepts) are divided into three categories, or *genders,* in German. They always start with a capital letter.

masculine (m.)	*feminine (f.)*	*neuter (n.)*
der Mann	die Frau	das Kind
der Bahnhof	die Apotheke	das Rathaus

The plural of nouns are formed in a variety of ways, but almost all feminine plurals end in **-en**.

2   **The definite article** (the) has masculine, feminine, neuter and plural forms to match the noun it is used with. These forms change according to the noun's function in the sentence:

- the *nominative* (dictionary form) shows the subject of a sentence
- the *accusative* shows the object (e.g. what you want, have, or are taking) and is also used after some prepositions e.g. **für**, **ohne**, **um**
- the *dative* is used after many prepositions e.g. **mit**, **nach**, **von**

	m.	*f.*	*n.*	*pl.*
nom.	der	die	das	die
acc.	den	die	das	die
dat.	dem	der	dem	den

Nominative:	**Der Fisch** ist gut.
Accusative:	Ich nehme **den Fisch**.
Dative:	Und mit **dem Fisch**?

3 The indefinite article **ein** (a/an) and the negative indefinite article **kein** (not a/not any) have the same forms, except that **ein** has no plural:

	m.	f.	n.	pl.
nom.	(k)ein	(k)eine	(k)ein	keine
acc.	(k)einen	(k)eine	(k)ein	keine
dat.	(k)einem	(k)einer	(k)einem	keinen

4 **Es gibt** (there is/there are) is a set phrase which is always followed by the accusative. When used with **kein** it means 'there isn't/there aren't'.

> Es gibt **einen** Marktplatz in der Nähe.
> Es gibt **keinen** Kaffee.   Es gibt **keine** Tomaten.

5 **Prepositions** (e.g. with, from, to) generally go in front of a noun and frequently specify location. Most prepositions are followed by the dative, e.g. **neben der Post**, but some are followed by the accusative, e.g. **um die Ecke**. Certain prepositions usually combine with the definite article. For example:

in dem Rathaus	→	**im** Rathaus
von dem Bahnhof	→	**vom** Bahnhof
zu dem Marktplatz	→	**zum** Marktplatz
zu der Post	→	**zur** Post

6 **Adjectives** are descriptive words. They change when used in front of a noun, but not when separated from it, so you are advised at this stage to follow the pattern of these examples:

> Das T-Shirt ist **teuer**.   Die Orangen sind **groß**.

7 **Er**, **sie** and **es** (see 9 **Verbs**) can refer both to people and to objects. This means that a masculine word such as **der Bahnhof** should be referred to as **er** and a feminine word such as **die Post** should be **sie**:

> Wo ist der Bahnhof?   **Er** ist hier rechts.
> Ist die Post hier links?   Nein, **sie** ist da drüben.
> Wo ist das Museum?   **Es** ist am Marktplatz.

This is a new concept for English speakers, and in the early stages you can always use **das** (that) instead:

Wo ist die Post? Das ist links.

8 There are three words for '**you**':

> **du** a friend, a member of the family, a young person
> **ihr** more than one of the above
> **Sie** the polite form, both singular and plural, used to address people you don't know well, but also with colleagues.

9 **Verbs** are words for doing, being or having. In English a verb is easily recognized because 'to' can be put in front: 'to work', 'to go', 'to be', 'to have'. The infinitive (dictionary form) of almost all German verbs ends in **-en**. Verb endings change according to who or what is doing the action, and most endings follow this regular pattern:

		kaufen to buy	**gehen** to go
I	ich	kaufe	gehe
you (s.)	du	kauf**st**	geh**st**
he/she/it	er/sie/es	kauf**t**	geh**t**
we	wir	kauf**en**	geh**en**
you (pl.)	ihr	kauf**t**	geh**t**
they	sie	kauf**en**	geh**en**
you (polite)	Sie	kauf**en**	geh**en**

Some verbs with a **t** or **d** before the **en** in the infinitive need an extra **e** in the **du**, **er/sie/es** and **ihr** forms to help pronunciation:

arbeiten (to work): du arbeit**est**, er/sie/es arbeit**et**, ihr arbeit**et**

An Umlaut (**ä**) is added to the **du** and **er/sie/es** forms of some verbs, affecting the sound (see Pronunciation guide, page 6):

fahren (to go/travel): du f**ä**hrst, er/sie/es f**ä**hrt

10 Irregular verbs don't follow the regular pattern and have to be learnt individually. The most commonly used are:

		sein to be	haben to have	können to be able to (can)	müssen to have to (must)
I	ich	bin	habe	kann	muss
you	du	bist	hast	kannst	musst
he/she/it	er/sie/es	ist	hat	kann	muss
we	wir	sind	haben	können	müssen
you	ihr	seid	habt	könnt	müsst
they	sie	sind	haben	können	müssen
you	Sie	sind	haben	können	müssen

Verbs following **können** and **müssen** are always in the infinitive form and come at the end of the sentence:

Kann ich einen Platz **reservieren**?
Sie **müssen** in Bonn **umsteigen**.

11 Separable verbs sometimes split into two parts:

ankommen (to arrive):	Wann kommt der Zug **an**?
abfahren (to leave):	Wann fährt der Zug **ab**?
umsteigen (to change):	Sie steigen in Stuttgart **um**.
aussteigen (to get off):	Ich steige in Basel **aus**.

But when used in the infinitive they do not split:

Muss ich **umsteigen**?
Sie müssen in Wien **aussteigen**.

12 As in English, **questions** can be asked by using a question word, such as:

wann?	when?		**wie?**	how?
was?	what?		**wo?**	where?
was für?	what kind of?		**woher?**	where . . . from?

In questions without a question word, the verb always comes first, followed by the subject (the person or thing who does the action):

Haben Sie Orangen?
Sind Sie verheiratet?
Muss ich umsteigen?

13 In **statements**, the verb always comes second. If the subject is not the first thing in the sentence, then it immediately follows the verb:

Ich **nehme** das Hähnchen.	Als Vorspeise **nehme** ich Suppe.
Der Zug **fährt** nach Wien.	Heute **fährt** der Zug um zehn Uhr.

14 **Nicht** (not) usually goes in front of what it is negating:

Der Zug fährt **nicht** nach München.
Der Parkplatz ist **nicht** weit.

German–English glossary

This glossary contains only those words and phrases, and their meanings, as they occur in this book. Parts of verbs are also given in the form in which they occur, followed by the infinitive in brackets.

A

der Abend *evening;*
    guten Abend *good evening*
    aber *but*
die Abfahrt *departure*
die Abteilung *department*
    acht *eight*
    achtzehn *eighteen*
    achtzig *eighty*
    alles *everything, all*
    alt *old*
die Altstadt *old (part of) town*
der Amerikaner *American man*
die Amerikanerin *American woman*
    an *at*
die Ananas *pineapple*
die Ankunft *arrival*
der Apfelkuchen *apple cake*
der Apfelsaft *apple juice*
die Apotheke *chemist's*
der April *April*
    arbeite (arbeiten) *(I) work (to work)*
    arbeitslos *unemployed*
der Architekt *architect*
    auch *also, too*
    auf Deutsch *in German*
    auf Wiedersehen *goodbye*
der Aufschnitt *cold meats*
der August *August*
    aus *from, out of*
die Auskunft *information*
der Ausländer *foreigner (m.)*
die Ausländerin *foreigner (f.)*
    aussteigen *to get off (transport)*
der Australier *Australian man*
die Australierin *Australian woman*

B

das Bad *bath*
der Bahnhof *(railway) station*
die Banane (pl. Bananen) *banana*
die Bank *bank*
die Bar *bar*
    Basel *Basle*
der Bayer *Bavarian (man)*
    bayerisch *Bavarian (dialect)*
    bei *(working) for*
der Beruf *occupation*
    besetzt *occupied*
der Besucher *visitor (m.)*
    bezahlen *to pay*
das Bier *beer*
    bin (sein) *(I) am (to be)*
    bis *until, to;*
        bis zum *until the (date)*
    bitte *please, don't mention it*
    bitte schön *here you are*
    bitte schön? *can I help you?*
    Bozen *Bolzano*
das Brötchen (pl. Brötchen) *(bread) roll*
der Brunnen *fountain*
das Büro *office*
der Bus *bus*
die Bushaltestelle *bus stop*

C

der Campingplatz *campsite*
der Cent *cent*
die Cola *coke (drink)*

D

    da *there*
der Dampfer *steamer*
    danke *thanks, thank you*
    danke schön *thank you (very much)*
    dann *then*
    darf (dürfen) *(I) may (to be allowed);*
        darf ich . . . ? *may I . . . ?*
    das *that, the (n.);*
        das ist *that is*
        das macht . . . *that comes to . . .*
        das sind *these are*
    der *the (m.)*
die Deutsche *German woman*
der Deutscher *German man*
das Deutschland *Germany*
der Dezember *December*
    die *the (f. or pl.);*
        die sind *they are, those are*
der Dienstag *Tuesday*
der Dom *cathedral*
der Donnerstag *Thursday*
das Doppelzimmer *double room*
    dort *there;*
        dort drüben *over there*
die Dose *tin, can*
    drei *three*
    dreimal *three times*
    dreißig *thirty*
    dreizehn *thirteen*
    dritte *third;*
        im dritten Stock *on the third floor*
die Dusche *shower*

E

    ebenfalls *likewise*
die Ecke *corner*
    ein, eine *a, an, one*
    einfach *single (ticket)*
das Einkaufszentrum *shopping centre*
    einlösen *to cash (a cheque)*
    einmal *once*

eins *one*
das Einzelzimmer *single room*
das Eisbein *knuckle of pork*
elf *eleven*
empfehlen *to recommend*
das England *England*
der Engländer *English man*
die Engländerin *English woman*
entschuldigen Sie *excuse me*
er *he*
das Erdgeschoss *ground floor*
erste *first;*
  die erste Straße *the first road*
  erster Klasse *first class (ticket)*
  im ersten Stock *on the first floor*
es *it;*
  es freut mich *pleased to meet you*
  es gibt *there is, there are*
  es tut mir leid *I'm sorry*
etwas *something, anything*
der Euro *euro*

F

die Fähre *ferry*
die Fahrkarte *ticket*
fahre (fahren) *(I) travel (to travel)*
fährt (fahren) *(it) travels (to travel)*
der Familienname *surname*
der Familienstand *marital status*
der Februar *February*
finde (finden) *(I) find (to find)*
der Fisch *fish*
die Flasche *bottle*
das Frankreich *France*
die Frau *wife, woman, Mrs*
die Frauenmode *women's fashions*
frei *free, vacant*
der Freitag *Friday*
fremd *strange*
der Freund (pl. Freunde) *friend*
freut mich *pleased to meet you*
frisch *fresh;*

frisches Obst *fresh fruit*
das Frühstück *breakfast*
fünf *five*
fünfzehn *fifteen*
fünfzig *fifty*
für *for*

G

das Gasthaus *pub*
gegenüber *opposite*
gehen (gehen) *(you) go (to go)*
das Geld *money*
gemischt *mixed;*
gemischtes Eis *mixed ice cream*
geöffnet *open*
geradeaus *straight on*
das Gericht (pl. Gerichte) *dish*
gern *I'd love to, willingly*
das Geschenk (pl. Geschenke) *present (gift)*
geschlossen *closed*
das Glas *glass*
das Gleis *platform*
das Gramm *gram*
groß *big*
Grüß Gott! *hello!*
gut *good, well;*
  gute Nacht *goodnight*
  guten Abend *good evening*
  guten Appetit! *enjoy your meal!*
  guten Morgen *good morning*
  guten Tag *good day, good afternoon*

H

habe (haben) *(I) have (to have)*
das Hähnchen *chicken*
halb *half;*
  ein halbes Kilo *half a kilo*
hat (haben) *(it) has (to have);*
  es hat gut geschmeckt *it was good*
  hat's geschmeckt? *did you enjoy your meal?*

der Hauptbahnhof *main station*
das Hauptgericht (pl. Hauptgerichte) *main course*
das Haus *house*
die Hausfrau *housewife*
die Haushaltswarenabteilung *household goods department*
heiße (heißen) *(I) am called (to be called)*
heißen (heißen) *(you) are called (to be called)*
helfen *to help*
der Heringssalat *herring salad*
der Herr *Mr*
heute *today*
hier *here*
hin und zurück *return (ticket)*
hinter *behind*
der Holländer *Dutchman*
das Hotel *hotel*
hundert *(a) hundred*

I

ich *I*
Ihnen *(to) you*
Ihr, Ihre *your*
im *in the (m./n.)*
in *in;*
  in der Nähe *nearby*
internationale *international*
der Ire *Irishman*
die Irin *Irishwoman*
das Irland *Ireland*
ist (sein) *(he/she/it) is (to be)*
der Italiener *Italian (man)*
die Italienerin *Italian (woman)*

J

ja *yes*
das Jägerschnitzel *pork cutlet with peppers and mushrooms*
das Jahr (pl. Jahre) *year;*
  . . . Jahre alt *. . . years old*
der Januar *January*
der Juli *July*
der Juni *June*

K

der Kaffee *coffee*
das Kalbfleisch *veal*
die Kalbsleber *calf's liver*
der Kanadier *Canadian man*
die Kanadierin *Canadian woman*
kann (können) *(I) can (to be able to)*
das Kännchen *pot, jug*
der Karton *carton*
der Käse *cheese*
der Käsekuchen *cheesecake*
die Kasse *till, cash desk*
das Kaufhaus *department store*
kein, keine *not a, not any*
die Kekse (pl.) *biscuits*
die Kellnerin (f.) *waitress*
das Kilo *kilo(gram)*
das Kind (pl. Kinder) *child*
der Kinderspielplatz *children's playground*
das Kirschwasser *cherry brandy*
klein *small*
der Knoblauch *garlic*
Köln *Cologne*
komme (kommen) *(I) come (to come)*
kommt . . . an (ankommen) *(it) arrives (to arrive)*
die Konditorei *cake shop*
der Kontrollpunkt *checkpoint*
kostet (kosten) *(it) costs (to cost)*
der Krabbencocktail *prawn cocktail*
die Kreditkarte *credit card*
der Kunde *customer (m.)*
die Kundin *customer (f.)*

L

das Land *country, German state*
langer Samstag *'long Saturday'*
langsam *slow(ly)*
die Lebensmittelabteilung *food hall*
die Leber *liver*
die Lederwarenabteilung *leather goods department*
der Lehrer *teacher (m.)*
die Lehrerin *teacher (f.)*
die Limonade *lemonade*
links *left, to the left*
der Liter *litre*
lokale *local*
das Lotto *Bingo*

M

der Mai *May*
man *you, one;*
man schreibt *you write/spell*
der Mann *man, husband*
die Männermode *men's fashions*
der Marktplatz *market square*
der März *March*
der Mechaniker (m.) *mechanic*
die Mechanikerin (f.) *mechanic*
mein, meine *my*
die Melone *melon*
mich *me*
die Milch *milk*
das Mineralwasser *mineral water*
das Minigolf *crazy golf*
die Minute (pl. Minuten) *minute*
mit *with, by;*
mit dem Bus *by bus*
mit der Fähre *by ferry*
die Mittagspause *lunch break*
der Mittwoch *Wednesday*
möchte (mögen) *(I) would like (to like)*
der Montag *Monday*
montags *on Mondays*
der Morgen *morning;*
guten Morgen *good morning*
München *Munich*
das Museum *museum*
muss (müssen) *(I) have to (to have to);*
muss ich . . . ? *do I have to . . . ?*
die Mutter *mother*

N

nach *to, towards*
die Nachspeise (pl. Nachspeisen) *dessert*
nächste *next*
die Nacht (pl. Nächte) *night;*
gute Nacht *goodnight*
der Name *name*
die Nationalität *nationality*
neben *next to*
nehme (nehmen) *(I) take, (I)'ll take (to take)*
nehmen (nehmen) *(you) take (to take)*
nein *no*
neun *nine*
neunzehn *nineteen*
neunzig *ninety*
nicht *not;*
nicht wahr? *isn't it? etc.*
nicht weit von . . . *not far from . . .*
nichts *nothing*
die Nieren (pl.) *kidneys*
noch *another, more;*
noch ein(en) . . . *another . . .*
sonst noch etwas? *anything else?*
der November *November*
die Nudeln (pl.) *noodles*
null *nought, zero*
die Nummer *number*
die Nusstorte *nut gateau*

O

der Ober *waiter*
das Obst *fruit*
oder *or*
ohne *without*
der Oktober *October*
die Orange (pl. Orangen) *orange*
der Orangensaft *orange juice*
das Österreich *Austria*
der Österreicher *Austrian man*
die Österreicherin *Austrian woman*

P

die Packung *carton*
das Päckchen *small pack, packet*
das Parfum *perfume*
der Parkplatz *car park*
der Platz *seat, square*
der Polizist *police officer (m.)*
die Polizistin *police officer (f.)*
die Pommes frites (pl.) *chips*
die Post *post office*
die Pralinen (pl.) *chocolates*
der Programmierer *computer programmer (m.)*
die Programmiererin *computer programmer (f.)*
Prost! *cheers!*

R

das Rathaus *town hall*
der Rathauskeller *town hall cellar (restaurant name)*
die Rechnung *bill*
rechts *right, to the right*
der Reis *rice*
der Reisescheck (pl. Reiseschecks) *traveller's cheque*
reservieren *to reserve, to book*
die Reservierung *reservation, booking*
das Restaurant *restaurant*
der Rinderbraten *roast beef*
das Rindfleisch *beef*
der Rotwein *red wine*
der Ruhetag *rest day*
das Rumpsteak *rump steak*

S

die Sahne *cream*
der Salat *salad*
der Samstag *Saturday;*
    langer Samstag *'long Saturday'*
    samstags *on Saturdays*
der Sauerbraten *braised beef marinated in vinegar*
der Schinken *ham*
das Schinkenbrötchen *ham roll*

der Schlüssel *key*
die Schokolade *chocolate, drinking chocolate*
die Schokoladentorte *chocolate gateau*
schon *already*
schön *nice*
der Schotte *Scottish man, Scotsman*
die Schottin *Scottish woman, Scotswoman*
schreibt (schreiben) *(one) writes/spells (to write)*
die Schreibwaren (pl.) *stationery*
das Schweinefleisch *pork*
das Schweinekotelett *pork chop*
die Schweiz *Switzerland*
das Schwimmbad *swimming pool*
sechs *six*
sechzehn *sixteen*
sechzig *sixty*
der Sekretär *secretary (m.)*
die Sekretärin *secretary (f.)*
der September *September*
sicher *certainly*
Sie *you*
sie *she, they*
sieben *seven*
siebzehn *seventeen*
siebzig *seventy*
sind (sein) *(we/you/they) are (to be)*
der Sohn (pl. Söhne) *son*
soll (sollen) *(I) should (to ought to);*
    soll ich ...? *should I ...?*
der Sonnabend *Saturday*
der Sonntag *Sunday*
sonst noch etwas? *anything else?*
der Spanier *Spanish man*
die Spanierin *Spanish woman*
die Speisekarte *menu*
die Spezialitäten (pl.) *specialities*
die Sportabteilung *sports department*

sprechen (sprechen) *(you) speak (to speak);*
    sprechen Sie langsamer! *speak more slowly!*
das Stadion *stadium*
die Stadtmitte *town centre*
das Stadttheater *civic theatre*
das Stehcafé *'standing café'*
der Steward *steward*
die Stewardess *stewardess*
der Stock *floor*
die Straße *street, road*
die Straßenbahn *tram*
der Student *student (m.)*
die Studentin *student (f.)*
suche (suchen) *(I)'m looking for (to look for)*
die Suppe *soup*
die Süßwarenabteilung *confectionery department*

T

das T-Shirt *T-shirt*
der Tag *day;*
    guten Tag *good day, good afternoon*
die Tagessuppe *soup of the day*
die Tasche *bag, handbag*
die Tasse (pl. Tassen) *cup*
der Tee *tea*
das Telefon *telephone*
die Telefonnummer *telephone number*
die Terrasse *terrace*
teuer *expensive*
die Tochter (pl. Töchter) *daughter*
die Toilette (pl. Toiletten) *toilet*
die Tomate (pl. Tomaten) *tomato*
das Tomatenbrötchen *tomato roll*
die Tomatensuppe *tomato soup*
die Trauben (pl.) *grapes*
tschüs *bye*
der Tunfisch *tuna*
der Tunfischsalat *tuna salad*

U

die U-Bahn *underground (train)*
die Uhr *o'clock*
    um *at, round*
    umsteigen *to change (transport)*
    und *and*
das Untergeschoss *basement*
die Universität *university*

V

der Vater *father*
    verheiratet *married*
der Verkäufer *sales assistant, salesman, stallholder*
die Verkäuferin *sales assistant, saleswoman, stallholder*
das Verkehrsamt *tourist information office*
das Verkehrsbüro *tourist information office*
der Verkehrsverein *tourist information office*
    verstehe (verstehen) *(I) understand (to understand)*
    vielleicht *perhaps*
    vier *four*
der Viertelliter *a quarter of a litre*
    vierzehn *fourteen*
    vierzig *forty*
    voll *full*
    vom … bis zum … *from the … to the …*
    von *from*
der Vorname *first name*

die Vorspeise (pl. Vorspeisen) *starter*
    vorstellen *to introduce, to make introductions*

W

der Waliser *Welshman*
die Waliserin *Welshwoman*
    wann? *when?*
das Warenhaus *department store*
    was? *what?;*
        was für …? *what kind of …?*
    wechseln *to change (money)*
der Wegweiser *store guide*
der Wein *wine*
der Weißwein *white wine*
die Weißwurst *Munich white veal sausage*
    weit *far*
    welche? *which?;*
        von welchem Gleis? *from which platform?*
        welche Linie? *which number/line?*
    werden Sie bedient? *are you being served?*
    wie? *how?;*
        wie geht es Ihnen?
        wie geht's? *how are you?*
        wie lange? *how long?*
    wiederholen (wiederholen) *(you) repeat (to repeat)*
        wiederholen Sie! *repeat it!*
    Wiedersehen *'bye*
    Wien *Vienna*

das Wiener Schnitzel *breaded veal cutlet*
    wir *we*
    wo? *where?*
    woher? *where from?*
    wohne (wohnen) *(I) live (to live)*
die Wurst *sausage*

Z

    zahlen *to pay*
    zehn *ten*
das Zimmer *room*
der Zimmernachweis *accommodation service*
    zu *to;*
        zu Fuß *on foot, walking*
der Zug *train*
        zum *to the (m./n.);*
        zum Trinken? *to drink?*
        zur *to the (f.)*
der Zuschlag *supplement*
    zwanzig *twenty*
    zwei *two*
    zweimal *twice*
    zweite *second;*
        die zweite Straße *the second road*
        im zweiten Stock *on the second floor*
        zweiter Klasse *second class (ticket)*
die Zwiebeln (pl.) *onions*
    zwo *two*
    zwölf *twelve*

Now you're talking!